The Cost of Staying

Find Your Courage, Choose Yourself, and Discover What Awaits in Life and Career

Kristen Chimack

Copyright © 2025 by Kristen Chimack

As You Wish Publishing

www.asyouwishpublishing.com

All rights reserved.

ISBN: 978-1-951131-79-1

Library of Congress Control Number: 2025903576

No portion of this book may be reproduced in any form without written permission from the publisher or author, except as permitted by U.S. copyright law.

Praise for The Cost of Staying

"As someone who left the corporate world to start a business over a decade ago, this is the book I wish I had read back then! Now, after building a community of thousands of women entrepreneurs, many of whom have made the leap from corporate to entrepreneurship, I'll be recommending this book to all of them. Kristen not only shares a deeply moving and relatable story, but she also provides a clear roadmap for navigating the emotions, challenges, and unexpected joys of choosing yourself.

Her Growth Through Grief framework perfectly captures what so many of our Entreprenista members experience but may struggle to put into words. And you're going to want to implement her virtual Diet Coke relationship building strategy, as it just may be the key to personal and professional growth in your next chapter. If you're standing at your own crossroads, wondering if there's more to life than climbing the corporate ladder, let this book be your permission slip that you, too, can create the life that you want and deserve."

— Stephanie Cartin, Co-Founder Entreprenista

THE COST OF STAYING

"This is a must-read for anyone navigating the corporate world feeling lost or alone. Through candid, relatable stories, this book reminds you that you're not the only one and offers practical guidance to help you find and build your own path toward joy and fulfillment. It's a powerful blend of truth, connection and hope".
— **Ashley Herd, Founder & CEO Manager Method**

"As someone who's built my career helping others forge their own path, I can say with certainty: Kristen's framework isn't just theory—it's a practical guide for anyone ready to choose themselves. Her Growth Through Grief model speaks to both men and women navigating major transitions, offering a refreshingly honest look at what it really takes to build something authentic. This book is essential reading for anyone who believes success shouldn't require sacrificing your soul."
— **Scott MacGregor, Publisher & Editor-In-Chief for Outlier Magazine, Founder of The Outlier Project's, Founder & CEO of SomethingNew LLC, 4x Author, Record 8x Winner of the American Business Award for Innovation**

A beautiful combination of personal and professional stories that will have you shaking your head in agreement and saying, "I've been there too." Kristen Chimack not only shares relatable stories from her decorated career but provides action-oriented exercises to help move you forward. The Cost of Staying: Find Your Courage, Choose Yourself, and Discover What Awaits in Life and Career is

PRAISE FOR THE COST OF STAYING

an easy-to-read and definitive guide to reinforce your belief in the power of showing up as your authentic self.
— **Laura Krauss, Author of The Layoff Cooties-It's Them, Not You and Founder of Ripple Effect Sales Advisory**

"*Kristen's story is one that can be found in all of us who participate in the corporate 9-5 hustle. Her experiences are unique to her, yet strikingly similar to those other professionals face. You'll find yourself in her story and through that, meaningful ways to accept, heal, and grow, intentionally silencing the noise and choosing yourself.*"
— **Elizabeth Taylor, Owner/CEO, The Corporate Bestie**

A Note To Readers

This book shares my personal journey, from family stories to three decades of corporate life. While my professional history is public, these experiences reflect challenges we all face in choosing authenticity over comfort.

What you'll read represents my memories and perspective. Names and details have been changed to protect privacy. Others may remember events differently - that's the nature of personal stories.

This is a story of growth, courage, and joy - about what I learned through choosing yourself and finding your way back to who you've always been.

For my grandma Gail, who taught me that being yourself wasn't just acceptable, it was essential, and my grandfather, who showed me the power of words. For my husband, who not only supported this crazy journey but asked the question that changed everything: "What's the worst that could happen?" And for my nieces and nephews, who remind me daily what authentic joy looks like. You've all made me a better person just by being exactly who you are.

And to my incredible community who showed up with virtual coffee chats, late night texts, and unwavering support, you proved that authentic connections create possibilities I never imagined. This journey of growth through grief became beautiful because of all of you.

Contents

Foreword	XIII
Introduction	XVII

Part 1: The Whispers

1.	The Decision to Choose Yourself	3
2.	The Power of Perspective	23
3.	The Surprise of Grief	37
4.	The Whispers Practice	53

Part 2: Letting Go

5.	The Art of Letting Go	65
6.	Nurturing Meaningful Relationships	77
7.	When "Work Family" Isn't Family	91
8.	The Practice of Letting Go	101

Part 3: Possibilities

9.	Redefining Success	111
10.	The Reality of Authentic Leadership	129
11.	The Joy of Choosing You	147

12. Possibilities Practice 157

Part 4: Integration

13. Embracing Authenticity 175
14. Living Your Truth: The Journey Continues ... 187
15. The Practice of Integration 195

Conclusion: The Journey Continues 209
Unsent Letters: The Words We Carry 213
About the Author 219

Foreword

What if you removed your past from your future? What freedom would that give you to move from a career that drains you to a calling that lights you up? Let that sink in.

This is the framework I wish I had in October 2022 when I felt completely lost. I had followed the expected path—college, corporate ladder, chasing promotions until reaching the C-suite. Yet, despite doing everything "right," I was living a life that wasn't aligned with who I truly was. My corporate journey yielded a divorce during COVID, toxic workplaces, and ultimately, the realization that joy awaited me on a different path.

The Growth through Grief Spiral that Kristen shares in ***The Cost of Staying*** offers a compassionate framework for navigating transformation. It begins with Listening to Your Whispers—those quiet moments when your inner voice tells you that you're meant for more. For me, that whisper was clear: "I don't want to go back. I am meant for more."

Next comes Letting Go, often the most painful part. You grieve the identities, roles, and beliefs that no longer serve you. For me, this meant detaching my self-worth from job titles. Who am I when I stop letting titles define my value?

Then comes the Possibility Phase, where glimpses of new opportunities emerge. Curiosity replaces fear as you explore what life could look like when you honor your truth. I realized that in my corporate roles, I wasn't using my full potential. Toxic environments encourage you to dim your light to fit in—but what if you stopped shrinking?

Finally, Integration brings it all together, weaving the lessons, joy, and possibilities into a life that's both meaningful and sustainable. Everything came together in my entrepreneurial journey when I combined my master connector superpowers with my deep desire to help others heal personally and scale professionally. This led to the creation of MY VIBE, a virtual community "shopping mall" designed for collaboration, reciprocity, and redefining commerce. I finally found a way to channel my passions and talents into building a better system—one rooted in integrity.

Through this journey, I discovered what I call "Blessons"—Blessings in your Lessons. When you lean into your core values, you naturally find yourself surrounded by people and opportunities that celebrate your innate gifts and make you feel worthy simply for being who you are.

Traditional careers often come with golden handcuffs—salary, benefits, retirement, and stability. But without boundaries, those handcuffs become a prison. What once felt secure can turn into a system where questioning the norm is seen as a threat. That's your first signal: you were meant for more. You feel it—but do you trust it?

If you're ready for GROWTH, then GRIEF will be part of the process, and you aren't alone. Kristen's framework will gently guide you through each step, showing you how transformation unfolds. You can't unsee it—and you won't want to.

No one can give you permission but you. The power to transform your life is yours alone—when you choose yourself.

Michelle Pecak, Founder of MYVIBE Community

Introduction

The Cost of Staying

I've lived an amazing life—truly. Growing up in the Midwest with a secure family, I've been fortunate enough to have never wanted for anything. My life was comfortable and stable. But that's not to say it hasn't been filled with pivotal moments—those defining crossroads that shape you in ways you never see coming. These moments, often born out of difficult choices or a feeling deep inside urging me to move forward, have left an indelible mark on who I am today. And in each of them, there's been a common thread: growth through grief.

It might sound strange at first, coupling those two ideas—growth and grief—but they are inseparable in my journey. You see, every significant moment of growth in my life has also come with a measure of grief. Grief over what I had to leave behind, over the person I once was, over the comfort I'd grown used to. But it's in those moments of loss—whether it's the loss of a relationship, a job, or simply the way things once were—that I've found the greatest growth.

Throughout this book, I'll share my story with you—the moments that defined me, the lessons I learned, and the choices that shaped my life. But this isn't just my story. It's a roadmap for anyone facing their own crossroads, complete with practical tools to help you navigate change with courage and clarity. You'll discover how to recognize toxic environments, maintain your authenticity in challenging situations, and make decisions aligned with your true values—not someone else's expectations.

You will also find two powerful tools to guide your journey. At the end of each chapter, you'll discover what I call "Aha! moments"—those game-changing realizations that hit you like a bolt of lightning, and suddenly everything clicks. Like when I realized I had been calculating the cost of leaving my job but had never calculated the cost of staying. Then, at the end of each major section—The Whispers, Letting Go, Possibilities, and Integration—you'll find practical exercises designed to help you apply these lessons to your own life. These tools work together with the Aha! moments providing insight, and the exercises offering concrete ways to put that insight into action. They're not just activities; they're stepping stones on your path to choosing yourself.

My hope is that these stories will resonate with you on your own journey, especially during times when you're faced with pivotal moments. I want to show you that growth can come from the hardest experiences and that choosing yourself isn't selfish—it's essential. Together, we'll explore how to build resilience, redefine success on your own terms, and create meaningful relationships that support your growth.

Maybe you're facing a decision that feels impossible, or maybe you're grieving the loss of something or someone in your life. Maybe you're stuck in a toxic work environment, questioning your career choice, or simply feeling that nagging sense that there has to be more to life. Wherever you are, I hope my story can offer some guidance, some comfort, and perhaps the courage to choose yourself and embrace the growth that's waiting for you—even if it's wrapped in grief.

This is the story of my growth in grief. A journey of choosing myself, over and over again, and finding joy on the other side. And more importantly, it's your guide to doing the same.

Part 1

Whispers

"It starts with a feeling—that subtle knowing in your gut when something's off or that there has to be more. Before every major change in my life, the whispers came first."

Growth Through Grief Spiral

The Whispers

Chapter One

The Decision to Choose Yourself

Why is choosing yourself so hard? From a young age, we're taught to put others first. Be nice. Share your toys. Don't be selfish. By the time we reach adulthood, this conditioning runs deep, making the act of choosing ourselves feel like a betrayal of these unwritten rules. But what if choosing yourself isn't selfish? What if it's the most important decision you can make?

Throughout my life, I've faced this question at pivotal moments—moments when the cost of putting others first became too great. That inner voice urging me to choose myself started as a whisper in my college years. During my freshman year, I saw a flyer for the Disney College Program. Something inside me stirred. I'd never even been to Florida, let alone Disney World. I had just started making friends, finding my rhythm in classes, creating a comfortable routine. The logical thing would have been to stay put, to not rock the boat, and to do what my parents expected.

But that voice whispered, "There's more out there for you."

My friends thought I was crazy. "Why would you leave when you're just getting started here?" My family was supportive but concerned that I might not return to finish college. But I went to the information session, interviewed the next day, and out of hundreds of applicants, I was one of 13 selected. That first choice to listen to the whisper changed everything. It was my first time away from home, my first time on an airplane, and my first taste of the wider world.

That same whisper led me to Bristol, England, for a summer international studies program in my junior year. Once again, the voices of doubt crept in. "You're just getting comfortable here. Why leave?" But I had learned to recognize that pull toward growth, even when it meant leaving comfort behind.

These early choices were like training wheels for the bigger decisions to come. Each time I chose myself—whether it was moving to a new state for work or taking on an entirely new role—that voice got a little stronger, a little clearer. But it wasn't until I faced three major crossroads that I truly understood the profound connection between choosing yourself, grief, and growth.

The 10-Year Relationship

For ten years, I was in a relationship that, from the outside, seemed perfect. We shared love, laughter, a home and had built a life together. But there was one fundamental disconnect—he didn't believe in marriage, and I did. Year after year, I convinced myself that love was enough and that I could let go of my dreams for our future. Deep down, though, I knew I was compromising a core part of myself.

I remember the moment I finally said it out loud: "One day, I will choose myself." The words came out before I even realized I was thinking them. He looked at me, surprised, maybe even a little hurt. But we both knew it was true. I had been hearing that whisper for years, trying to ignore it, trying to make peace with a future that didn't align with my deepest wants.

That choice was excruciating. Letting go of someone you've built a life with, even when you know it's for the best, comes with its own special kind of grief. I grieved not just the relationship but the future I had imagined, the comfort of having someone there, the identity of being part of a couple, and the possibility of having kids. But in that grief, just like with Disney and England, I found my strength. I grew. I chose me.

But that wasn't all I lost. Mutual friends felt they had to choose sides, and suddenly, people who had been a part of my life for years faded away. The house we'd made our home had to be sold, forcing me to say goodbye to the physical space that held so many memories. It was gut-wrenching, and for a while, I felt unmoored, like I had lost everything familiar.

Yet, in that grief, I discovered something profound: I was stronger than I thought. Letting go of him allowed me to make space for a future that aligned with my true desires. I began to rebuild my life on my own terms, and in the process, I found a deeper sense of self.

> **Reflection Moment**
> Take a breath here. Think about a time when you stayed in a situation longer than you should have because it was comfortable, even though something felt misaligned. Maybe, like me, you told yourself, "It's good enough" or "I can make this work." Notice how your body feels when you think about that situation. That tension? That's your inner wisdom trying to tell you something. Sometimes the hardest choices come disguised as the most logical ones to everyone else.

Each of these moments built upon the last, teaching me something crucial about choosing myself. The Disney decision taught me to trust that inner whisper. England showed me that growth often means leaving comfort behind. Ending the relationship taught me that choosing yourself sometimes means standing alone.

The Executive Meeting: A Turning Point

The signs had been there for years in my corporate career, though I tried to ignore them. Early on, a female executive pulled me aside and suggested I should "dumb it down" because being intelligent intimidates others. She even added, with what I'm sure she thought was a helpful concern, that maybe if I did that, I'd find a husband. "That will be important," she said, "if you want to become an executive at this company."

I should have left then. The wise version of me today sees that so clearly. But I loved this company. They were woven into the fabric of my life, my identity, my sense of security. The company prided itself on statements like "we're a family," "titles don't matter," and "we want your opinion." Beautiful words written on walls and repeated in meetings. But the reality? "Family" meant sacrificing your personal life without question. "Titles don't matter" really meant "don't challenge those above you." And "we want your opinion"? That came with an unspoken caveat: as long as it aligned with what leadership already thought.

Then came the meeting that changed everything. It was a Monday during a holiday week, and I was already juggling a flurry of texts and emails, trying to keep the wheels turning in a toxic environment. When I was called into a meeting with one of our executive leaders, I knew something was off.

"We know how bad it is," they said that day, acknowledging the dysfunction that had been weighing on me for years. But instead of offering a solution, they asked me to help prop it up. I was to "coach" my struggling boss and quietly absorb the burden. The final blow came when they asked, "Do you still want to be in an executive role?" The implication was clear: play along, or risk everything.

Walking back to my office after that meeting, my mind was racing. But beneath all the thoughts about next steps and practical implications, something deeper was shifting. The people I had worked alongside for 20 to 30 years—people I had fiercely defended whenever they were criticized—were now asking me to prop up the very dysfunction that was suffocating me.

That's when it hit me: I couldn't pretend anymore, not just about this situation, but about any of it. All these years of carefully managing messages, of trying to be "strategic" in my communication, of playing the corporate game while telling myself I was being authentic—it was over.

The very qualities they'd once praised me for—my directness, my drive for truth, my unwillingness to accept the status quo—were now being seen as threats. Not because I'd changed, but because I'd finally stopped trying to make my authenticity palatable to a system that only wanted the appearance of truth, not the real thing.

In that 30-minute conversation, all the trust I had built over 30 years was shattered. No one was going to help me but me.

The voice inside me screamed, "Choose you." It was no longer a whisper but a roar. Staying would mean betraying my values and continuing to sacrifice my well-being. That moment crystallized everything I had been grappling with: my time there was coming to an end. The cost of staying was far greater than the fear of leaving.

When I finally decided to leave, the company's messaging worked overtime to keep me in place: "You won't find these benefits elsewhere." "No one leaves at your level." "You're too old to start over." But that voice inside me, the same one that had guided me to choose myself before—with Disney, with England, with ending my relationship—was getting louder. And it was saying something different: "You've outgrown this." "Your mental health is worth more than a paycheck." "You have so much more to offer." "Choose you... again."

Leaving came with immense loss. I didn't just walk away from a job—I left behind colleagues who had become like family. People I had traveled with, celebrated wins with, and leaned on during difficult times no longer spoke to me. The organization I had poured my heart into, one that had felt like home, had betrayed me. And when I finally left, I felt like a stranger to myself. The identity I had built over 30 years was gone.

But in that void, I found something more valuable: freedom. Freedom to redefine my life, to explore who I was outside of my title, and to prioritize my health and happiness. The grief was heavy, but the growth that followed was transformative.

> **Reflection Moment**
>
> Remember a time when someone asked you to compromise your values "for the greater good" or "to be a team player." How did it feel in your body? What did that inner voice tell you? Like my experience, these moments often come wrapped in familiar language: "helping others," "being strategic," and "thinking of your future." But beneath those words usually lies a simple truth: you're being asked to be less than who you are.

The Financial Reality of Choosing Yourself

You know what nobody tells you about choosing yourself? Sometimes, it means completely rewriting the financial story you've been telling yourself for decades.

I had it all mapped out—work until 65, collect my pension, enjoy a comfortable retirement. It was the responsible plan, the safe plan, the one everyone expected. But life has a funny way of showing you that your carefully crafted plans might not align with what you need.

In my early 40s, I started making small adjustments. Maybe 65 was too long to wait—what about 62? I increased my 401K contributions and bumped up my personal savings. Look at me being so practical, I thought. I was still following "the plan," just with a slightly earlier end date.

But then something started stirring in my late 40s. That whisper or gut feeling we talked about earlier? The one that said "choose you"? Well, it started getting louder when it came to my future. The culture at work was shifting, and not in a good way. I found myself dreaming about doing something different, something that aligned more with my values. That's when I made another adjustment to the plan—leave at 55, start a second career.

Still responsible, right? Still had a plan. Just needed to figure out what that second career would be. I started putting away a little more money, just in case. Fewer dinners out, one less vacation each year. Small sacrifices that felt like insurance for my future freedom.

But here's the thing about toxic environments—they have a way of accelerating your timeline whether you're ready or not. As the expectations at work became more demanding and the culture more draining, it became crystal clear that waiting until 55 might cost me more than just money. My mental health was suffering. My joy was disappearing. No paycheck is worth that price.

That conversation with the executive leader didn't just cement my decision to leave—it forced me to really look at what I valued more: financial security based on someone else's timeline or the freedom to choose my own path. The paycheck, the salary, the benefits—they were golden handcuffs, and I had to decide if the price of wearing them was worth it.

It still took nine months after that meeting to actually turn in my resignation. Nine months of running numbers, adjusting budgets, and having hard conversations with myself and my spouse about what security really means. My husband and I had always lived below our means, but this would be a significant change. Together, we had to redefine what financial security looked like and decide if the cost of staying was worth more than the risk of leaving.

The conversations with my husband weren't just about money—they were about identity and partnership. He'd known me for most of my corporate career. He'd seen the toll it was taking, watching me daily grow more frustrated and drained. But he'd also seen me thrive there in earlier years. During one particularly emotional discussion, he asked me something that changed everything: "What's the worst that could happen?" We played out every scenario—from wild success to having to go back to corporate life. And none of the "worst case" scenarios seemed as bad as staying in the current situation.

We made practical decisions, too. We looked at our mortgage, our savings, our spending habits. Could we live on one income if we needed to? What about health insurance? Each question led to an action plan. We built a financial cushion that could support us through the transition. Not just emergency savings, but what I called my "freedom fund"—money specifically set aside to give me the runway to build something new.

The irony wasn't lost on me—I had spent years helping manage multi-million dollar budgets at work, yet calculating my own road to freedom felt far more challenging. But just like those corporate budgets, this was about allocating resources to what mattered most. The difference? This time, I was investing in myself.

But this wasn't the first time I'd had to trust my instincts about choosing myself, even when it meant facing financial uncertainty. Those early decisions had been preparing me for this moment. Each choice to choose myself built upon the last, creating a foundation of trust in my own judgment.

Setting Boundaries with a Friend

Choosing yourself doesn't just happen in romantic relationships or careers; it's often just as difficult with friendships. One of my closest friends (let's call her Kami) was struggling with alcohol, and her negativity began seeping into every interaction. We'd been friends for over fifteen years, sharing life's ups and downs, celebrating victories, and supporting each other through tough times. But gradually, our relationship shifted from mutual support to me becoming her lifeline.

It started subtly. A few extra glasses of wine at dinner turned into showing up to lunch already tipsy. Late-night phone calls asking for advice became 2 AM crisis interventions. What began as occasional venting about life's frustrations transformed into constant negativity about everything and everyone—her job, her family, mutual friends, even the weather.

I tried everything I could think of to help. I researched treatment options. I adjusted my schedule to be available whenever she needed me. I even started turning down other social invitations, knowing Kami might call needing help. My own anxiety grew as I constantly checked my phone, wondering if she was okay, if today would be the day something terrible happened.

The breaking point came after a particularly rough weekend. Kami had called me five times in one night, each call more emotional than the last. By Monday morning, I was exhausted, having barely slept. As I sat in an important meeting at work, my phone buzzing with her messages, I realized something had to change. I wasn't just failing to help her—I was hurting myself in the process.

After a difficult conversation with her family, where we all fought back tears, I explained I could no longer be her safety net. "She's my best friend," I told them, "but I can't keep catching her when she falls. She needs professional help, and I need to step back to protect my own well-being." Setting that boundary was one of the hardest things I've ever done. I grieved the friendship we once had and wrestled with guilt. Would she be okay? Was I abandoning her when she needed me most?

And once again, the losses rippled out. Our mutual friends drifted away, unsure how to navigate the space between us. Some thought I was being cruel, not understanding the full story. Others awkwardly tried to maintain relationships with both of us, eventually giving up because it was too complicated. The vibrant, supportive network we'd built together fractured. I found myself mourning not just one friendship, but a whole community.

The hardest part was the silence. After years of constant communication, the absence of her messages felt deafening. I'd catch myself reaching for my phone to share something funny or interesting, only to remember we weren't speaking. Mutual friends would slip and mention her name, then quickly change the subject, leaving an awkward void in the conversation.

But even as I navigated this painful transition, I found strength. Without the constant drain of managing Kami's crises, I had energy to invest in other relationships. I started sleeping better. My anxiety decreased. I rediscovered hobbies I'd let slide while being on constant call for her. Most importantly, I learned that loving someone doesn't mean sacrificing your own well-being for them. Sometimes, the most caring thing you can do—for both yourself and the other person—is to step back and let them find their own way.

Yet, even now, years later, I occasionally question my decision. I've heard through mutual friends that Kami finally got help, and that she's doing better. Part of me wonders if I could have handled things differently. But then I remember the toll it was taking on my life, how I was enabling rather than helping, and I know I made the right choice. Letting go allowed me to focus on relationships that were healthier and more balanced. It taught me the importance of setting boundaries, even when it hurts, and reaffirmed that protecting your peace is not selfish—it's necessary.

This experience changed how I approach all my relationships. I learned to recognize the early warning signs of unhealthy dynamics. I became better at communicating my boundaries before situations became critical. Most importantly, I understood that choosing yourself doesn't mean you don't care about others—it means you care enough about yourself to maintain healthy boundaries.

> **Reflection Moment**
> Think about a relationship in your life where caring for someone else has started to mean caring less for yourself. Notice how your shoulders feel right now. Your chest. Your stomach. Our bodies often know before our minds catch up that something needs to change. Sometimes, the most loving choice—both for ourselves and others—is to step back, even when that choice breaks our hearts.

Growth Through Grief

In all three of these moments, I lost something significant—a partner, a career, and a friend. But the losses didn't stop there. I lost mutual friends, a sense of belonging, and pieces of my identity. I lost a home, a professional community, and the comfort of familiar routines. Each choice felt like it stripped away a layer of my life, leaving me raw and exposed.

It was hard. It was gut-wrenching. And yet, it was necessary.

Through the pain, I learned that growth and grief are deeply intertwined. Every loss created space for something new. I grew stronger, more resilient, and more aligned with my authentic self. I learned that choosing yourself is not about avoiding loss—it's about having the courage to face it, knowing that on the other side lies a version of you that is truer, freer, and more at peace.

The Growth Through Grief Spiral

Through these experiences—the relationship, the career, the friendship—I discovered something fascinating about choosing yourself. It's not the neat, linear path everyone promises, where you make a decision, deal with the fallout, and move on. Instead, it's more like a spiral staircase. You might pass the same spot multiple times, but each pass gives you a new perspective and a deeper understanding.

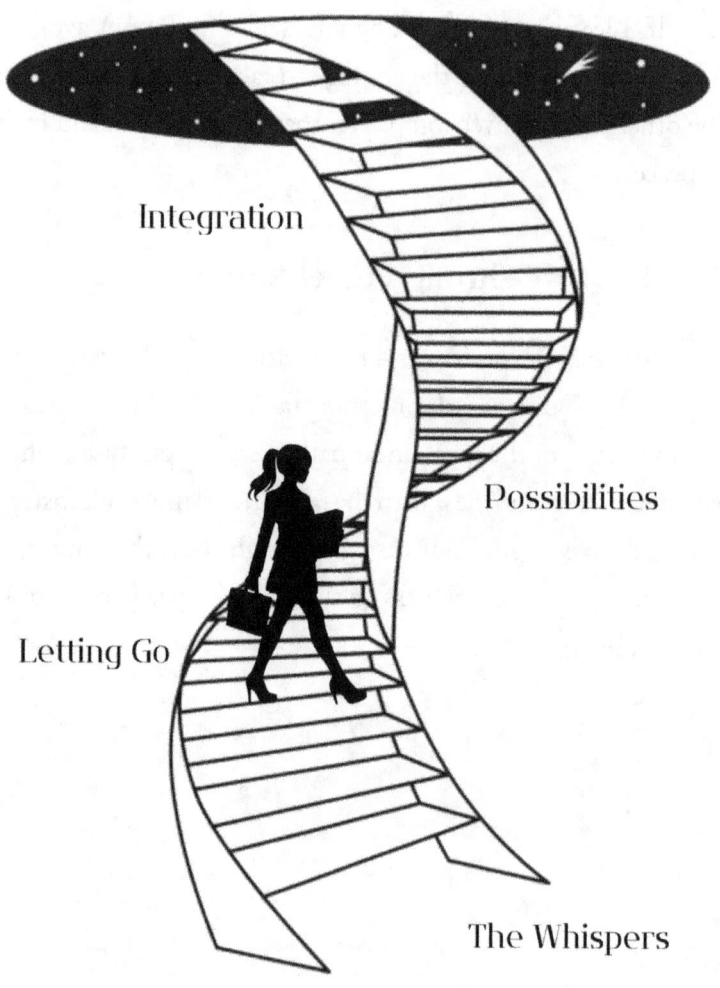

Let me share the spiral that emerged from my journey—one that's helped me understand not just my own path but also guided others through their transformations. I call it the Growth Through Grief Spiral, and it has four distinct phases:

The Whisper Phase This is where that inner voice first speaks up, like that whisper of "choose you" I kept hearing. It's your body keeping score before your mind catches up. Remember how I felt physically ill walking into the office? Or how my anxiety spiked every time Kami called? That's your inner wisdom at work. It's when your gut knows what your head isn't ready to admit.

The Letting Go Phase This is where you start peeling away layers: old identities, others' expectations, and what you thought your life "should" look like. Think about how I had to release not just my executive role but my whole identity as a corporate leader. Or how, with Kami, I had to let go of the idea that I could save her. Letting go isn't just about what you're leaving; it's about making space for what's coming.

The Possibility Phase This is where you start seeing doorways where there used to be walls. Like when I realized I could redefine success on my own terms, or when ending that 10-year relationship opened me to finding a partnership that truly aligned with my values. New possibilities emerge in the space that letting go creates.

The Integration Phase This is where grief and growth dance together, creating something new. It's where all those seemingly separate choices—from choosing Disney to leaving corporate America—start weaving together into a more authentic life. You start seeing how each choice to choose yourself was actually preparing you for the next one.

Here's the thing about this spiral: you don't just go through it once, and you're done. With every choice to choose yourself, whether big or small, you may move through these phases multiple times. But each time, you do it with more wisdom, more trust in yourself, more understanding of the process.

Sometimes, you might spiral through all four phases quickly, like when setting a small boundary. Other times, like with my corporate career, you might spend months or even years moving through different phases. That's okay. This isn't a race; it's a journey back to yourself.

But here's something important about this spiral: choosing yourself doesn't always have to come with such high stakes. Sometimes, it's about the small, everyday decisions that remind you of your worth. It's taking a pajama day when you need to recharge. It's scheduling that long-overdue massage. It's saying yes to a weekend getaway or giving yourself permission to sit on the couch and binge your favorite show without guilt.

These small moments matter. They're like practice rounds with the spiral. You listen to that soft voice telling you what you need, let go of the guilt about taking time for yourself, open up to what feels good, and bring these small acts of self-care into your daily life. They teach you how to listen to your needs, how to prioritize your well-being, and how to honor yourself even in the midst of life's chaos. They're the building blocks that prepare you for the bigger decisions. Every time you choose yourself—whether in a life-changing decision or a quiet, personal act—you're reinforcing the belief that you are worthy of care, love, and attention.

Looking back now, I can see how each choice to choose myself built upon the last. From those early decisions to leave for Disney and study in England to ending a decade-long relationship to walking away from a successful career to setting boundaries in friendships—each time I chose myself, that inner voice got stronger. Each time through the spiral, I gained new insights, new courage, and new understanding. What started as a whisper became a steady guide, leading me back to who I truly am.

So, whether you're standing at a major crossroads or simply deciding how to spend your Sunday, remember this: Choosing yourself is an act of courage, no matter the size. And while moving through the spiral may bring grief, it always leads to growth.

Aha! Moment

I used to think choosing myself meant being selfish. But one day, sitting with my leadership coach, listing all the reasons I couldn't leave my executive role—the paycheck, the security, my reputation—she asked one simple question: "But what's the cost of staying?"

That's when it hit me. I had spent years calculating the cost of leaving, but I had never truly calculated the cost of staying. I was so focused on what I might lose by leaving that I couldn't see what I was losing by staying—my authenticity, my peace of mind, my joy, my health. The biggest cost wasn't financial at all; it was the price of not choosing myself, over and over again.

In that moment, I realized choosing yourself isn't selfish—not choosing yourself is. Because when you don't choose yourself, you're not only diminishing your own light but also teaching others to do the same. Sometimes, the most courageous thing you can do is admit you need help and take that first step toward change, even if you can't see the whole path ahead.

Chapter Two

The Power of Perspective

They say time gives you perspective, but honestly, sometimes perspective hits you like a ton of bricks before you're ready for it. That's what happened to me in those final months at my corporate job. One minute, I was deep in the daily drama, and the next... well, let's just say seeing clearly isn't always comfortable.

When Rose-Colored Glasses Shatter

The hardest part about gaining perspective is that it forces you to see something you've loved your whole life in a completely different light. This wasn't just a company I worked for—it was woven into the fabric of my childhood, my family, my entire life story.

My dad worked there for most of my life before I did. When I think back to my childhood, this company is everywhere in my memories: the kids' holiday parties where I got my first glimpse of Santa, the summer day camps where I made friends, the family events that dotted our calendar year-round. Most of my friends' parents worked there, and later, my friends would work there too. This wasn't just a workplace—it was my community, my extended family, my home.

For over 30 years, I believed in this company with my whole heart. I knew the senior leaders both personally and professionally. When employees would come to me over the years with stories about toxic environments or unfair treatment, I was the cheerleader for the company. "Talk to your leadership," I'd say. "Go to HR—they'll help make it right." I genuinely couldn't believe these horrible things could be happening in the company I loved so deeply.

I was like that friend who keeps defending an unhealthy relationship because they can't bear to see the truth. "You just don't know them like I do," I'd think. "There must be more to the story."

But as I started to choose myself and show up authentically in my last few years there, something strange happened. Those stories I'd dismissed? I started experiencing them firsthand. All those things I thought couldn't possibly be true? They were unfolding right in front of me. It was like putting on glasses for the first time and suddenly seeing all the cracks in what I thought was a perfect picture.

The more I pushed for positive cultural change, the more the culture began to reject me. It's funny how that works—the moment you start questioning the system, the system starts questioning you. I began to realize this wasn't the company I had grown up with and loved. It wasn't really a family. The leaders protected each other and those they considered friends—though "friends" really meant people they needed to continue moving up the ladder.

As this perspective settled in, I found myself moving further and further outside their circle. The people creating the toxic environment—where women were expected to do more than men, where discrimination was tolerated, and incompetence was rewarded—were all part of this inner circle. They were all friends, and here I was, calling out one of their friends with concrete, documented proof of the problems.

The First Cracks in the Foundation

You know how sometimes you notice a small crack in something, and suddenly you can't stop seeing it? That's how it started for me. Little things at first—the way certain leaders would say one thing in town halls but do another behind closed doors. How the women in leadership roles were held to different standards than their male counterparts. How "open door policies" seemed to close pretty quickly when someone raised real concerns.

I remember this one moment vividly. A female colleague (let's call her Lily) came to me in tears after being told she was "too aggressive" in meetings. The thing is, I'd been in those same meetings. She wasn't aggressive; she was competent and direct, just like our male colleagues. But when they spoke up, they were "confident leaders." When she did it, she was "aggressive."

Years ago, I might have told Lily to work on her communication style or suggested she talk to HR. But this time, something clicked. I remembered all those other women who'd come to me over the years with similar stories—stories I'd dismissed or explained away. Now I was seeing it happen in real-time, and I couldn't unsee it.

The Childhood Memories Shift

What really got me was how this new perspective started coloring even my childhood memories. Those company Christmas parties I'd loved so much? I started remembering other details—how it was always the women facilitating these events, organizing everything, making sure it all ran smoothly while the men networked. The summer camps? I realized now they existed not as some wonderful perk but because the company expected such dedication that parents needed somewhere for their kids to go when school was out. Heaven forbid employees actually take vacation time to be with their children during the summer.

But the hardest shift came in how I viewed my dad's 40 years at the company. During those years, I'd viewed his long hours as dedication and commitment—something to be proud of. Now I saw something different: all the moments missed, the dinners he wasn't there for, the events he couldn't attend. What I had viewed as admirable dedication, I now recognized as time we could never get back.

Even the family events I'd treasured took on a different hue. Yes, they brought people together, but they also created this sense of obligation to the company. "We're family" started to sound less like a warm embrace and more like a chain keeping people tethered to a bad environment. The company wasn't creating family moments—it was replacing them with company-sanctioned substitutes for the real family time we were all missing.

The Loyalty Tax

I started noticing what I came to think of as the "loyalty tax"—the price people paid for staying loyal to the company. And let me tell you, this tax came in many forms.

The longer you stayed, the more you were expected to sacrifice. Your personal time? That belonged to the company. Your boundaries? Those were seen as a lack of commitment. Your authentic voice? That needed to be modulated to match what leadership wanted to hear.

But here's the kicker—there was also a literal price to our loyalty. While we stayed put, committed to the company, they were paying us significantly less than what similar roles earned at other companies. The justification? "We offer stability." That was their favorite line: "We don't do layoffs like other companies." It was a masterful manipulation when you think about it. They had us believing we should be grateful for making less money because, hey, at least we had job security.

I now know that "stability" was really golden handcuffs. They used it to keep people from looking elsewhere, to make us feel like we were trading fair market wages for security. And the longer you stayed, the harder it became to leave. Your skills became company-specific, your salary fell further behind market rates, and the pension golden carrot kept dangling just a few more years away.

The Daily Grind of Toxicity

Working in a toxic environment where you have no idea who you can trust is an all-consuming, exhausting experience. My days usually started with people texting me or waiting for me to come into the office—simply to complain about something or to talk about someone. In the moment, it felt like we were supporting each other, that we understood the challenges, and that we were fighting a common enemy for the good of the department or cause.

But as I began to distance myself in the final nine months before resigning, something shifted. Maybe it was because I'd finally seen through the façade of "family" the company had maintained all these years. Maybe it was because I could no longer pretend things would get better if I just tried harder. Whatever the reason, I started seeing these daily interactions in a whole new light.

The Uncomfortable Clarity

Remember how I used to tell employees to go to HR or leadership when they had problems? Well, now I was the one raising issues, armed with documentation and concrete examples. And you know what happened? The same thing that had probably happened to all those employees I'd sent down that path years ago—nothing. Worse than nothing, actually. I was told to stop pointing out problems and help maintain the very dysfunction I was fighting against.

I started seeing things differently. I began to question whether we were ever really on the same team. Yes, we all wanted things to improve, but it became clear that "improve" meant different things to different people. Some wanted change without having to change themselves. Others wanted problems fixed but weren't willing to be part of the solution.

The Friend Fallacy

One of the hardest realizations was coming to terms with the fact that the very people I had trusted, shared personal things with, and was vulnerable with—those I believed were my friends—had used that information to their own advantage. These weren't just colleagues; these were people I'd grown up with in the company, people whose kids I knew, people I'd celebrated holidays with for decades.

It became clearer with time that many of those I had supported and championed weren't friends at all. They had used me to fight their battles—battles they were too scared or unwilling to take on themselves. Just like the company had used the idea of "family" to keep people in line, I realized these relationships had been built on convenience rather than genuine connection.

I see now how they would complain to me, knowing I would take it forward, thinking I was fighting the good fight for everyone. But in reality, it was their fight all along, not mine. And rather than face the challenges head-on, they gossiped in private, complained to one another, and let me carry the weight of it publicly.

When I stepped away, I could finally see how they would embrace the very people they had criticized if they thought it would benefit them or discard others the moment they were no longer useful. It was like watching a play I'd been performing in for years, only now I was in the audience, seeing all the staged moments for what they really were.

The Mean Girls Moment

With perspective came the harsh realization that I had allowed myself to be used and manipulated. I had been pulled into middle-school-like "mean girl" behaviors—something I never thought I would experience in the corporate world, let alone in a company I'd once believed could do no wrong. And yet, there I was.

I let my desire to help and my belief in our so-called friendships cloud my judgment. Just like I had spent years defending the company against criticism, I had spent years making excuses for behaviors that should have raised red flags. I was scared of what would happen if I pulled away, of the isolation that might come. But stepping away has shown me that the real isolation came from staying in the destructive dynamic.

When Perspective Leads to Power

Once you see things clearly, you actually gain power—even if it doesn't feel that way at first. When I finally understood that the "stability" the company offered was really just a beautiful cage, something shifted. I started making different choices.

I began setting boundaries around my time. When those late-night requests to create PDFs came in, I waited until morning to respond. When weekend work was "suggested," I started saying no. I turned my computer off at 4:30—something that would have been unthinkable before. I even started using my vacation time instead of letting it pile up while I worked endless hours.

All those back-to-back meetings where everyone complained, but nothing changed? Well, I started declining them. "Sorry, I have another commitment" became my new favorite phrase, and sometimes that commitment was simply to my own well-being. Surprisingly, the world didn't end. In fact, something unexpected happened: some of my team members started doing the same thing. It was like they'd been waiting for permission to set their own boundaries.

My voice got louder, too. In meetings, I stopped playing the diplomatic game. If something didn't make sense, I said so. If a decision seemed questionable, I asked why. When I saw women being talked over or their ideas being co-opted by male colleagues, I spoke up. "Actually, that was Jane's idea from last week's meeting. Jane, would you like to expand on your original thought?" The looks on people's faces when I did this—priceless.

I got bolder about addressing the toxic environment, speaking up not just in meetings but taking my concerns to the highest levels of leadership. One conversation in particular revealed something I'll never forget. When I shared what was happening, the response stunned me - they weren't even surprised. In fact, they admitted hearing about these issues through neighborhood party gossip. Let that sink in for a minute. Senior leadership knew how bad things were through social circles and still did nothing. They were aware but chose inaction.

That moment was another perspective shift all its own. Here I was, thinking I was finally bringing these issues to light at the highest level, only to discover they were party conversations. But instead of feeling defeated, I felt liberated. The last threads of obligation I felt toward "fixing" the culture snapped. I realized I wasn't failing to create change; the system was working exactly as those in power wanted it to work.

This new clarity changed how I showed up in every way:

- I started documenting everything, not to protect myself, but to have concrete examples when people tried to gaslight me about the environment.

- I began connecting directly with other women in the organization, sharing resources and creating informal support networks.

- I stopped trying to make others comfortable with my truth.

- I quit filtering my feedback through the lens of "How will this land?"

- I started planning my exit openly, not hiding the fact that I was exploring other options.

Yes, this directness probably accelerated my exit, but it also showed me who I could become when I stopped playing by rules designed to keep me small. Each tiny act of rebellion, each boundary set, each truth spoken—they were all steps toward choosing myself.

The Space Between Seeing and Grieving

There's this interesting space that exists between gaining perspective and processing what that perspective shows you. It's like standing in a doorway. You can see both where you've been and where you need to go, but you haven't quite stepped through yet.

When you start seeing clearly, grief isn't far behind. You grieve for the illusions you've lost, for the time you can't get back, for the person you were before you knew what you know now. But here's what I've learned: this grief isn't a burden; it's a bridge. It's taking you somewhere important.

The company I'd loved since childhood? The relationships I thought were unshakeable? The success I'd defined by their standards? All of it needed to be grieved before I could fully step into what was next. And that's okay. Sometimes, seeing clearly is just the first step in a longer journey of letting go.

With this new perspective came an unexpected companion: grief. Not just for what I was leaving behind, but for the illusions I'd held onto for so long.

Aha! Moment

My most powerful Aha! moment came during a regular Tuesday afternoon meeting. Everyone was doing the usual dance: nodding along, sending furious IMs about their real thoughts, planning the "meeting after the meeting" to complain about what was being decided. I looked around the room and suddenly saw it all with crystal clarity: I wasn't stuck here. I wasn't trapped by the pension, the stability, or the relationships. The only thing keeping me here was my own inability to let go of who I thought I needed to be.

In that moment, I realized perspective isn't just about seeing clearly; it's about being willing to act on what you see. Just like that moment years ago when I chose myself by going to Disney or when I ended that 10-year relationship, this new perspective wasn't just showing me what was wrong; it was showing me what I needed to do about it.

Chapter Three

The Surprise of Grief

Leaving a place where you've spent decades is tough. When I think back to that executive meeting, I'm struck by how much grief was packed into those thirty minutes. It wasn't just grief over the eventual loss of my position; it was grief for the death of illusions I'd held onto for years. But the truth is, the grief had started long before that meeting. I just didn't recognize it for what it was.

Grief, I would learn, has its own way of speaking—first through your body, then through your emotions, and finally through a clarity that changes everything.

The Slow Erosion

It started with colleagues. People I'd trusted, worked alongside, laughed with for years. Little by little, I began noticing how conversations would change when certain leaders walked into a room and how the same people who complained privately would nod enthusiastically in meetings. How information I shared in confidence would mysteriously make its way up the chain.

The distance grew slowly at first. I started being more careful about what I shared. Began choosing my words more carefully. Found myself holding back in conversations that used to flow freely. Trust, once broken, is like a crack in a windshield—it only spreads.

Then came the leadership betrayals. That meeting wasn't really the beginning; it was just the moment when I couldn't ignore what I'd been feeling for months or even years. Each time leadership chose politics over people, chose appearance over authenticity, chose convenience over truth, another piece of my trust crumbled.

Looking back now, I can see how my body and instincts were trying to tell me something before my mind was ready to hear it.

Understanding Professional Grief

Unlike personal grief, which is often acknowledged and supported, professional grief can feel isolating and "inappropriate." In the corporate world, we're expected to move on quickly and be "professional" about our losses. But the grief that comes from leaving a long-term career is both real and complex.

When I first tried to explain my feelings to friends, they seemed puzzled. "But you chose to leave," they'd say. "You're building something better." What they didn't understand was that you can be excited about your future while mourning your past. Professional grief doesn't follow the rules we've been taught about loss.

It took time to recognize what I was feeling as grief. A conversation with my coach finally put it into perspective. I was listing off all these physical and emotional symptoms—the sleepless nights, the random tears, the anger, the confusion—when she gently said, "Kristen, this sounds like grief."

I actually laughed. Grief? But I chose this. I was happy I left. This was what I wanted!

She just smiled and said, "You can be right where you're supposed to be and still grieve what you left behind."

When Corporate Culture Makes Grief Taboo

Corporate culture often makes grief feel taboo. We celebrate people's departures with forced smiles and cake in the break room, pretending that fifteen, twenty or thirty years of relationships can be neatly wrapped up in a two-week notice period. We're expected to maintain "professional boundaries" even as we process deep personal losses.

The same corporate environment that contributes to our need to leave also makes it harder to process that leaving. We're taught to be "resilient," to "adapt to change," to "maintain composure."

These very expectations can make the grief feel like a personal failure rather than a natural response to loss.

For years, I'd watched colleagues leave. We'd give them the standard farewell lunch, share memories over sheet cake, and promise to stay in touch. But no one ever talked about the grief. No one mentioned the confusion of walking away from decades of relationship building, the disorientation of losing your professional identity, and the strange mix of relief and loss that comes with choosing to leave.

The Body's Early Signals

Just like those initial whispers telling me to choose myself, my body started sending signals long before my mind caught up. In those first few months after leaving, I found myself:

- Obsessively checking my former company's social media

- Having anxiety dreams about work months after leaving

- Feeling defensive when people asked about my career change

- Experiencing unexpected emotional reactions to industry news

- Avoiding certain places or people that reminded me of my previous role

- Feeling compelled to justify my decision to leave
- Struggling with my professional identity in social situations

These reactions weren't just random responses; they were my body's way of processing what my mind wasn't ready to face yet. They were early signals of deeper changes taking root.

The Unraveling

Looking back, I can see how I was preparing for departure long before I made the conscious decision to leave. It started with my office. One day, I found myself taking home the family photos from my desk. The next week, it was the awards and memorabilia I'd collected over thirty years. Little by little, I was erasing myself from that space. No one noticed.

The unraveling of my professional identity happened in quiet moments. Eight months before I resigned, I began the digital equivalent of packing up my desk—removing work connections from my personal social media platforms. First, it was the people I knew were toxic. Then, those I wasn't sure I could trust. Finally, anyone connected to work. Each unfriend, unfollow, and disconnection felt like both a loss and a relief.

Questions began to surface that I couldn't push away: Were these relationships ever real? Did they ever care? Was it all an act? The more I questioned, the more I realized that what I thought were genuine connections might have been built on something far more fragile than I'd imagined.

But the real identity crisis hit after I left. Here is what's really humbling. That first networking call after leaving your executive role. For thirty years, it had been so easy: "Hi, I'm Kristen, Executive of [department] at [company]." The title did all the heavy lifting. It gave me instant credibility, opened doors, and set the tone. Now? I felt like I had to justify myself and explain my worth. It reminded me of those early moments choosing myself—leaving for Disney, moving to England—except this time, I wasn't just choosing a new experience; I was choosing a whole new way of being.

Those first few months, my introductions were a mess. I'd ramble on: "Hi, I'm Kristen. I was an executive at [company] for thirty years, but I left to start my own business, and now I'm doing coaching and hotel sourcing..." I could see people's eyes glazing over on Zoom calls. I was so afraid of being judged, of people thinking I'd failed or couldn't hack it in corporate anymore, that I felt compelled to explain my entire career history in the first breath.

The turning point came during a virtual coffee when my conversation partner gently interrupted my lengthy introduction and asked, "But who are you really?" It stopped me in my tracks. Who was I without the title? Without the corporate identity? It was a question I needed to answer not just for others, but for myself.

Now, as I help other leaders navigate their own transitions, I see them struggling with this same identity crisis. Just last week, I was working with a client who spent the first fifteen minutes of our call listing her achievements and titles, almost desperately trying to prove her worth. I heard myself in her words and saw myself in her need to justify her existence beyond her corporate role.

When Truth Emerges

The truth came slowly, like a heavy fog lifting, revealing things I hadn't wanted to see but could no longer avoid. I began seeing how I'd been used as the voice they needed because I was willing to speak up when they wouldn't. The fury wasn't just about them—it was about finally seeing the system for what it was, and my role in maintaining it.

You know those moments in movies where someone's memory flashes back, and suddenly everything looks different? That's what happened to me. Meetings I'd sat through years ago played back in my mind with new clarity. All those times I'd defended the company's decisions, explained away behaviors, and convinced others to stay—I wasn't just participating in the system; I was helping perpetuate it. Each memory brought a fresh wave of understanding, and with it, a deeper layer of grief.

My body was processing these truths before my mind caught up. Sleep became elusive—I'd wake at 3 AM, mind racing with conversations I wished I'd handled differently. My back, which had never given me trouble before, started acting up. Headaches became frequent visitors. Even my stomach got into the act, rebelling against the stress I was carrying.

But it was the exhaustion that really got me. Not the normal tiredness that comes from a busy day but a bone-deep weariness that no amount of sleep seemed to touch. My doctor said it was my body processing years of accumulated stress—like a sponge finally being allowed to release all the tension it had absorbed.

The truth wasn't just about seeing the organization clearly—it was about seeing myself clearly, too. All those times I'd told others to "work within the system," to "be more strategic" in their communication, to "play the game better"—I wasn't helping them. I was teaching them to shrink themselves just as I had learned to do. The realization hit hard: in trying to help others navigate a toxic system, I'd become part of the machinery that kept it running.

Each truth brought its own physical reaction. When I remembered coaching a young woman to "be less direct" in meetings, my stomach would clench. When I thought about all the times I'd advised others to "be more political," my jaw would tighten. My body was keeping score of every revelation, every moment of clarity about my role in the very system I'd eventually leave.

These physical manifestations weren't just symptoms to be managed; they were messengers helping me understand just how much truth I'd been holding back, how much reality I'd been denying. Like a computer processing years of backed-up data, my body was finally dealing with all the compromises, all the moments of choosing politics over truth, all the times I'd swallowed words that needed to be spoken.

When Relationships Change

In personal relationships, there's usually some form of closure: a final conversation and a chance to say goodbye. But in the professional world, relationships often end with the click of a mouse, the gathering of belongings, and a final walk through security.

The silence was deafening. These were people I'd traveled with, shared life milestones with, and spent more time with than my own family some weeks. We'd celebrated each other's kids' graduations, supported each other through divorces and deaths, and shared inside jokes that no one else understood. Now? Nothing. No calls, no texts, no responses to my messages. Just silence, or worse—questions about me passed through mutual friends. "How is she doing?" they'd ask, as if my phone number hadn't stayed the same for decades.

The hardest part wasn't just losing the relationships—it was questioning whether they were ever real to begin with. Those late-night conversations during business trips, the shoulders offered during tough times, the shared victories and defeats—were they just corporate convenience dressed up as friendship? It's like discovering your favorite photo is actually a filter—the warmth and depth you thought were real were just digital effects.

I still rehearse scenarios in my head. What happens when I run into these people around town? Our city isn't that big. Will we do that awkward dance of pretending not to see each other? Will one of us suddenly find the cereal aisle fascinating to avoid interaction? Or will we fall into that strange corporate autopilot: "Hey! How are you? We should catch up sometime!" knowing full well we won't.

Sometimes I catch myself drafting messages I'll never send: "Remember when we promised to always have each other's backs? What changed?" or "I miss our Thursday coffee chats. Do you?" But then I remember—just like those corporate values painted on walls, maybe these relationships were more about the appearance of connection than the reality of it.

When Loss Becomes Real

Grief seeps into every corner of your day. Three months after leaving, I still reached for my phone at 7:30 AM, expecting to check team messages. I'd catch myself mentally preparing for Monday morning meetings that no longer existed. My body remembered a routine my mind knew was over.

Driving around my city became an obstacle course of memories. I started taking different routes just to avoid driving past the office. But sometimes, I'd forget and end up sitting at that familiar stoplight, staring up at the building where I'd spent countless hours of my life. Once, I actually pulled into the parking garage out of habit before realizing what I was doing. The security guard's puzzled look in my rearview mirror as I quickly reversed felt like a perfect metaphor—I didn't belong there anymore.

The whole city became a map of memories I had to navigate. That coffee shop where we had our leadership meetings—where we'd strategized, celebrated, and sometimes cried. That restaurant where we celebrated promotions—the exact table where one of my employees got the news about their promotion to a director role. That hotel where we hosted events—the lobby where we rehearsed our presentation until 2 AM because he was so nervous. Each place held echoes of a life I'd left behind, stories that now felt like they belonged to someone else.

Even my home office betrayed me. The awards on my walls that once felt like achievements now felt like artifacts from a past life. The company logo on my favorite coffee mug became something I had to turn away from each morning. My professional wardrobe hung in my closet like costumes from a play I'd finished performing.

When Integration Begins

The real turning point came about six months after leaving. I was sitting in my home office when I got another notification that someone from my old company had viewed my LinkedIn profile. As usual, no message, no connection request—just silent watching from afar. But this time, instead of feeling that familiar mix of anger and sadness, I felt... something new. Not nothing exactly—more like peace.

That's when I realized something important: The grief wasn't just about losing them; it was about losing who I used to be. The person who trusted implicitly. The person who believed in corporate values painted on walls. The person who thought thirty years of loyalty meant something. That person was gone, and maybe that wasn't such a bad thing.

Like in earlier moments of choosing myself, this transformation wasn't just about what I was leaving behind. It was about who I was becoming. The person who emerged wasn't just older or wiser; she was more authentic, more aligned with her truth, more willing to stand in her own power.

I began to see how every lost relationship made space for new, more genuine connections. Every abandoned routine created room for more meaningful habits. Even those LinkedIn profile views took on a different meaning—maybe they weren't just watching out of curiosity, but because they saw someone choose themselves and wondered if they could do the same.

The Power of Professional Grief

Grief, I discovered, isn't just an obstacle to overcome—it's actually a doorway to transformation. Each experience stripped away another layer of corporate conditioning, making space for something more authentic to emerge.

The unraveling of my professional identity, though painful, was preparing me for renewal. The truth awakening, while uncomfortable, was teaching me to trust my instincts again. The relationship reckoning was showing me what genuine connections look like. Professional mourning was clearing the way for new possibilities. And integration? That was the beginning of true transformation.

Here's something I rarely admit: alongside the grief came guilt. Guilt about the things I didn't miss—those late-night emergency calls about font choices, the political navigation of who to copy on emails, the endless meetings about meetings. The guilt wasn't about missing these things; it was about not missing them. Shouldn't I miss it all? Wasn't that more loyal somehow?

Then there was the guilt about feeling grief at all. I'd chosen this. I was building something exciting. I was free from the toxicity. So why did it still hurt? Why did I care that these people who'd shown their true colors weren't reaching out? Why did it matter that they viewed my social media but never engaged?

The Physical Journey

Eventually, my body began showing signs of healing. Sleep came easier. The back pain subsided. The headaches became less frequent. It was like my body finally got the message that it was safe to relax, safe to let go, safe to be in this new reality.

Looking back now, I can see how grief was actually a kind of guide, showing me:

- What I truly valued (authentic relationships over superficial connections)

- What I really wanted (meaningful work over impressive titles)

- Who I actually was (separate from my corporate identity)

- What success really meant to me (not what the company had taught me it should mean)

Grief might feel like an ending, but I've learned it's actually a doorway. It's that space between who you were and who you're becoming. Sometimes, the very things that break our hearts are showing us what needs to change.

Aha! Moment

Grief is a strange thing. Just when you think you're doing better, something can pull you right back in.

I was lying in bed one night, tossing and turning, replaying an evening with girlfriends. Earlier, they'd mentioned running into a former colleague I'd been close with. "She asks about you all the time," they said. "She's worried about you. You really should reach out."

I tried explaining that I had reached out. Multiple times. With no response. But they were insistent. "There must be some misunderstanding. You two were such good friends. You've been through so much together."

After a couple of glasses of wine and some tears about missing our friendship, they convinced me. Maybe they were right.

Maybe it was all just a big misunderstanding. So I sent a text, opening my heart one more time. I shared how one of the hardest parts of leaving was losing our friendship. How much I missed our conversations. How I hoped she was doing well.

And then... nothing. No response. Not even a thumbs up. Not even a "Thanks, but no thanks." Just silence.

That's when it hit me. I wasn't just grieving the loss of my job or my identity. I was grieving these friendships. And here I was, starting that grief all over again. The whispers of doubt, the need to let go, the hope for something different, the struggle to find peace. The cycle was beginning again.

Sometimes, growth through grief isn't a straight line forward. Sometimes, it's more like a spiral, where you pass the same point multiple times, each time with a new understanding. And sometimes, the hardest part isn't the initial loss; it's accepting that what you thought was real might never have been real at all.

Chapter Four

The Whispers Practice

Remember how we talked about those quiet signals that something needs to change? Those moments when your body knows before your mind catches up? We've explored how these whispers guided me through choosing myself, shifting perspective, and navigating grief. Now, it's time to develop your ability to recognize and trust these signals. Think of this chapter as creating your personal early warning system, one that brings together all the elements we've discussed: listening to your inner voice, gaining new perspective, and honoring grief as it arises.

Your Whispers Workbook

Exercise 1: The Quick Three

Time needed: 15 minutes daily for one week

Think back to the executive meeting I told you about? The one where my body was screaming "something's wrong" even as my mind tried to rationalize? That's what we're learning to notice here.

Step 1: Check In (5 minutes) Grab your journal and quickly answer:

- What's bugging me lately? (First three things that pop up)
- Where am I making excuses? (Be brutally honest)
- What would I do if I wasn't afraid? (Dream big)

Step 2: Body Scan (5 minutes) For each answer above, notice:

- Where do you feel it in your body?
- What physical sensations arise?
- Rate the intensity (1-10)

Step 3: Pattern Recognition (5 minutes) At the end of each week, review your daily notes:

- What themes emerge?
- Which situations consistently trigger physical responses?
- What patterns do you notice in your excuses?

Now that you're learning to notice these signals, let's connect them to something deeper—your core values. Just like I had to learn that my tension headaches weren't just about stress but about misalignment with my values, you'll discover your body's unique language for telling you when something isn't aligned with what matters most.

Exercise 2: Core Values Discovery

Time needed: 45 minutes

Step 1: Values Brainstorm (15 minutes) Look at the core values chart. Listen to your inner wisdom, just like that voice that told me, "Choose you."

- Circle ones that make you feel energized
- Cross out any that feel like "shoulds"
- You may have to go through the list a few times to narrow it down to 5 that really resonate with you

My Core Values

Circle the three to five core values that resonate with you the most!

Honesty	Tolerance	Pleasure
Integrity	Open-mindedness	Self-awareness
Loyalty	Forgiveness	Self-acceptance
Compassion	Generosity	Self-confidence
Empathy	Courage	Independence
Respect	Perseverance	Freedom
Kindness	Determination	Family
Positivity	Ambition	Friendship
Accountability	Citizenship	Love
Gratitude	Innovation	Empowerment
Humility	Adaptability	Equality
Responsibility	Flexibility	Inclusivity
Trustworthiness	Curiosity	Diversity
Fairness	Wisdom	Environmentalism
Patience	Self-discipline	Sustainability
Collaboration	Adventure	Community
Teamwork	Education	Health
Excellence	Knowledge	Well-being
Quality	Learning	Exploration
Service	Justice	Faith
Altruism	Simplicity	Honor
Reliability	Balance	Unity
Authenticity	Resilience	Transparency
Creativity	Harmony	Spirituality
Openness	Peace	Fun

Step 2: Values Testing (15 minutes) For your top 5 circled values:

- When do you feel most aligned with this value?

- When do you feel it is being violated?

- How does your body respond in each case?

Step 3: Values Integration (15 minutes) Create your values compass:

- Write each core value

- List specific behaviors that honor it

- Note physical signals that indicate alignment/misalignment

With your values identified and your body's signals mapped, let's add another crucial tool—the ability to shift perspective. Remember how my view of success completely changed once I stepped back and looked at it differently? That's what we're doing here.

Exercise 3: Perspective Flip

Time needed: 30 minutes

Step 1: Choose Your Challenge (5 minutes) Pick one situation from your Quick Three that feels most pressing.

Step 2: View Shifting (15 minutes) Examine your situation through different lenses:

Time-Travel View

- How will this matter in 1 year?
- What would my future self advise?
- What would my past self think?

Friend View

- What would I tell my best friend?
- How would I support them?
- Why is it easier to give advice than to take it?

Growth View

- What's this teaching me?
- How might this prepare me?
- What's possible because of this?

Step 3: Integration (10 minutes)

- What new insights emerged?
- Which view felt most helpful?
- What action does this inspire?

As we've seen throughout these chapters, grief often accompanies growth. These next tools help you recognize and honor grief's role in your journey.

Tools for Noticing Grief

Throughout this section, I've shared how grief showed up in my world—in my body, my relationships, and even my driving routes around the city. Like those early whispers of "choose you," grief often speaks to us first through small signals:

Your Body's Whispers Keep a small note in your phone about:

- When tension shows up
- What triggers it
- What brings relief
- How your sleep changes
- What helps you feel steady again

Your World's Clues Notice changes in:

- Places you naturally avoid
- New routes you're taking
- Where memories hit hardest
- Spaces that feel safe

Your Relationships Shifts Pay attention to:

- Who's gone quiet
- Who's shown up
- What you miss most
- What you're learning about friendship

Signs of Growth Each week, catch one:

- New truth you've discovered
- Small change you notice
- Moment of unexpected peace
- Sign you're healing

Grief might feel like an ending, but I've learned it's actually a doorway. It's that space between who you were and who you're becoming. Sometimes, the very things that break our hearts are showing us what needs to change.

Bringing It All Together: Your Whispers Toolkit

Time needed: 15 minutes

Create your whispers reference guide that brings together all we've explored:

1. Your choosing yourself signals (from Quick Three)

2. Your values compass (from Core Values Discovery)

3. Your perspective-shifting tools (from Perspective Flip)

4. Your grief recognition patterns (from Grief Tools)

Remember: Just like my journey from those first whispers about choosing myself through perspective shifts to acknowledging grief; this is a practice. Some days, the signals will be clear; other days, they'll feel faint. That's okay. Keep listening. Keep noting. Keep choosing you.

Next Steps

- Choose one practice from Quick Three to do daily this week
- Post your Values Compass where you'll see it often
- Schedule time for weekly perspective checks
- Start your grief recognition journal
- Plan your first monthly review of all your tools

Your whispers are your inner wisdom speaking. The more you practice listening—whether it's about choosing yourself, gaining new perspective, or honoring grief—the clearer they'll become.

Ready to move into letting go? The next section will help you release what's no longer serving you, just like I had to release my corporate identity to make space for something new.

Visit www.kristenchimack.com for digital resources and to subscribe to the Kickin' it with Kristen newsletter

Part 2
Letting Go

"Nobody tells you that choosing yourself sometimes means walking away from everything you thought you wanted. This is about the courage to let go, even when you can't see what's next."

Growth Through Grief Spiral

Letting Go

The Whispers

Chapter Five

The Art of Letting Go

Sometimes a single conversation changes everything, even if we don't recognize its full impact in the moment. Just as I moved through earlier transitions—from that first leap to Disney to studying abroad in England to ending that 10-year relationship—that had taught me to trust my inner voice, now that same voice was guiding me through the complex process of letting go. While those earlier choices had been about moving toward something new, this transition required something different: the courage to release what was familiar, even when I couldn't yet see what would replace it.

This time, however, the voice spoke through a different kind of moment. Nine months before I officially resigned, that meeting with the executive initiated a cascade of letting go that would unfold in ways I never anticipated. The message had been clear: Help prop up the dysfunction. Support my struggling boss at all times. Stop sharing how bad things were, even though they knew and were aware. We were choosing him for promotion, no matter what.

The meeting with the executive might have been the catalyst, but looking back, I can see how my entire journey had been preparing me for this moment of release. Each time I had chosen myself—from walking away from that comfortable relationship to redefining success on my own terms—I had been practicing the art of letting go in smaller ways.

The Start of Letting Go

Letting go, I discovered, happens in layers—some quick and decisive, others slow and subtle. In those months between the meeting and my resignation, I began a gradual process of disconnection. Even as I continued showing up for work each day, I was unconsciously preparing for departure.

But while the physical letting go moved quickly, the emotional release followed its own, more complex timeline. Some relationships ended abruptly with my resignation, while others required conscious choices about boundaries and engagement. The deeper work—processing the anger, betrayal, and disillusionment—was just beginning.

Looking back now, I can see how letting go followed the same spiral pattern that had guided me through other transitions. Each phase is built upon the last, creating a deeper understanding of what it truly means to release what no longer serves us.

The Whisper Phase came through my body's wisdom. Even before my conscious mind was ready to acknowledge the need for change, my physical self was preparing for departure. The gradual clearing of my office—removing photos, throwing out awards, cleaning out files—these weren't just random acts. I even stopped attending company events and gatherings. They were my inner wisdom already knowing what needed to happen, whispering, "It's time" in the language of small actions.

The Letting Go Phase happened in layers, like peeling an onion. First came the physical items: those water bottles, t-shirts, and, yes, that perfectly broken-in company sweatshirt. Each item carried memories: team celebrations, project launches, and moments of triumph. What struck me was how these objects, which had once seemed so meaningful, now felt like artifacts from a past life.

Then came the digital ties—removing connections from social media, archiving old emails, and clearing out my phone contacts. With each "unfriend" or "unfollow," I felt a mix of sadness and relief. These weren't just digital housekeeping tasks; they were small acts of choosing myself, of creating distance from the toxicity I needed to leave behind.

Finally came the hardest layer: the emotional attachments and anger that had built up over the years. Each disconnection felt like cutting a thread that had once seemed vital but now felt like it was holding me back. Sometimes, I'd pause mid-cleanup, holding an old team photo or award, wondering if I was making the right choice. But my body knew. The relief I felt with each item cleared, each connection severed, was my inner wisdom confirming I was on the right path.

The Layers of Anger

You know what nobody tells you about letting go? Sometimes, the hardest part isn't the physical stuff; it's dealing with the anger you didn't even know you were carrying. For me, that anger came in waves, each one revealing another layer of truth I needed to face.

Like sediment in a riverbed, it had built up layer by layer, each new betrayal adding to its weight. At first, my anger focused squarely on leadership. I was furious about the environment that had been created, where women were treated differently than men, where being a "team player" meant covering for those who were struggling, where discrimination was tolerated, and we worked around the clock while some were allowed to remain unresponsive to all communications.

The anger wasn't just about current events—it was about recognizing how much of my identity had been wrapped in an illusion. Just as I had discovered in my journey toward authenticity, the very things that made me successful in the corporate world—my directness, my drive for truth, my unwillingness to accept the status quo—were now being seen as threats.

Then my anger shifted to HR and the executives—the very people who should have been protecting us. They would ask how I was doing, share their own frustrations with leadership, and even acknowledge the horrible environment. "Are you hanging in there?" they'd ask, as if they were powerless observers rather than leaders with the authority to make changes. To this day, I struggle to understand why none of them took action when it is their job to protect employees.

Finally, my anger turned toward the company itself. This wasn't the organization I'd known and trusted my entire career. The betrayal cut deep—this place that had been like family now felt like a stranger. Their repeated message to "Coach him, help him" felt like a cruel joke, as if they were all watching us try to navigate this toxic environment they'd created, perhaps even laughing at our attempts to make it work.

The Withdrawal and Understanding

As the anger grew, I withdrew. Trust became impossible—even when I tried to extend it, I was quickly shown why I shouldn't. Each attempt at vulnerability was met with another betrayal. The anger ran so deep that it began to color every interaction, every decision. Simple meetings became exercises in restraint. Casual conversations felt loaded with hidden meanings. Even emails required careful analysis—who to copy, what to say, how to phrase things to protect myself.

But nearly a year after leaving, something unexpected happened. As I gained distance from the situation, I started to see those involved differently. One leader was in a role they hadn't asked for, leading an area they knew nothing about, living in a city they probably didn't want to be in. Their own boss had worked around them from the beginning, treating them more like an obstacle than a leader, and they'd likely been given little to no direction. The truth began to dawn on me: they didn't have a chance... just like I didn't have a chance.

This realization didn't excuse the environment that had been created. The discrimination, the unfair treatment of women, the constant expectation to be available 24/7 while some were able to remain unresponsive—none of that was okay. But understanding that they, too, were caught in the dysfunction helped me begin to release the weight of anger I'd been carrying. It wasn't about forgiveness—it was about seeing the larger truth of a broken system that trapped everyone within it, even those who appeared to have power.

The understanding didn't stop there. As my perspective shifted, I began to see how others were trapped in this dysfunction, too—including those closest to me. One had mastered the art of manipulation. Their tactics were subtle but effective: isolating relationships, playing people against each other, making others too afraid to challenge them. I watched as they expertly maneuvered through the political landscape, leaving everyone hesitant to stand up to them.

The signs had been there from the start—how they would share confidential information to create alliances, how they would praise people publicly while undermining them privately, and how they positioned themselves as the only solution to problems they often created. But what I now understood was that their behavior wasn't just about power—it was about survival in a toxic system. They had found their way to navigate it, just as I had tried to fight it. Different responses to the same broken environment. This realization helped me release some of the anger I'd carried about their actions, too. The system hadn't just failed me—it had failed all of us, just in different ways.

This understanding wasn't just about release; it was creating space for something I couldn't yet see. Just as redefining success had opened new possibilities, letting go of anger and blame would create room for unexpected joy. The same pattern of growth through grief that had guided my earlier transitions was working again, though in a deeper, more profound way. Each layer of understanding peeled away another layer of resentment, making space for something new to emerge.

The Practice of Active Choice

This growing understanding shaped how I handled the practical challenges of letting go. Just as I had learned to trust my instincts in earlier transitions, my body once again became my guide. Four months after leaving, I attended a girls' weekend with friends. From the start, they were working on and off, constantly complaining about the organization and the people there. My body's response was immediate and visceral: tension in my jaw and racing heart, followed by nightmares about being back at work.

The next morning, still shaken from the dreams, I decided I needed to choose myself again. These weren't just casual conversations—they were pulling me back into the very toxicity I'd walked away from. I was beginning to realize that sometimes the hardest choices aren't about what we're moving toward but what we need to release. I had two choices: find new topics of conversation or step away from these gatherings entirely.

The conversation that followed wasn't easy, but it was necessary. "I care about you all," I explained, "but I can't keep reliving the workplace drama. It's affecting my health, my sleep, my peace of mind." Some understood and made an effort to change the conversation topics. Others seemed unable to talk about anything else—their identities were still too wrapped up in the corporate world. This moment echoed earlier lessons about authentic relationships—sometimes growth means letting people find their own path, even if it diverges from yours.

This was the Growth Through Grief Spiral in action again, recognizing what wasn't serving me (those conversations about work drama), letting it go (setting new boundaries), and making space for something better (deeper, more authentic connections). Each time, the choices got a little easier, even if they weren't always comfortable.

The Unexpected Gifts

The gifts show up in the most unexpected ways, kind of like finding money in an old jacket pocket, except what you find are pieces of yourself you'd forgotten existed.

First came the physical relief—and I mean *physical*. One morning, about three months after leaving, I realized I hadn't had a tension headache in weeks. My jaw wasn't clenched. I wasn't mentally rehearsing confrontations in the shower (please tell me I'm not the only one who does this!). Instead of spending energy managing my anger about the situation, I could actually focus on building something new.

The real gift? Clarity. It's like when you finally clean your glasses after walking around with smudges all day—suddenly, everything comes into focus. I could see situations and relationships for what they really were, not what I needed them to be. Those colleagues who'd seemed supportive? I could finally see how they'd actually been enabling the dysfunction. The mental energy I'd spent being angry? Now, it was available for creation and growth.

Then came this incredible sense of freedom. How much energy does it take to hold onto blame? To keep track of who did what and why they were wrong? Letting go of that need to assign blame (while still acknowledging what happened) felt like putting down a boulder I'd been carrying uphill. I wasn't excusing anyone's behavior, but I wasn't letting it occupy space in my head rent-free anymore, either.

But perhaps the most unexpected gift was renewed trust—not in others initially, but in myself. Each time I honored my own truth, set a boundary, or chose what was right for me, I rebuilt trust with the most important person: myself. It's like that trust muscle got stronger with every choice, creating a foundation for bigger leaps of faith.

The deepest gift was understanding—not just of others, but of myself. Seeing how everyone, even those I'd been angriest with, was caught in the same dysfunctional system gave me a more nuanced view of organizational dynamics. This insight has been invaluable in my coaching work. I can help others navigate similar situations because I've been there, but also because I understand there are no villains, just humans trying their best in broken systems.

Aha! Moment

The strangest part about letting go? Sometimes, the relationships you think will endure don't, and connections you never expected become meaningful in new ways. After I resigned, just like when I ended that long-term relationship years before, the aftermath of who showed up (and who didn't) surprised me.

I was touched when people reached out to share how I'd impacted their careers or expressed regret that we hadn't worked more closely together. These messages often came with invitations for breakfast, lunch, or drinks. At first, I said yes to everything. Some of these connections were genuinely about moving forward, but others? They were fishing expeditions to understand why someone would leave after 30 years or opportunities to share their own stories of dysfunctional bosses and difficult situations.

Initially, I welcomed these conversations. They validated my experience and my decision to leave. But one day, after a particularly heavy lunch discussion about ongoing workplace drama, I realized I was reliving my own trauma with every conversation.

Each story of toxicity and dysfunction pulled me right back into that environment I'd worked so hard to leave.

That's when it hit me: Sometimes, maintaining certain relationships means staying tethered to old pain. Just because someone reaches out doesn't mean we need to keep replaying the past. I started being clear upfront: "I'd love to meet, but I want to be honest: I'm not comfortable discussing my previous employer. I'd rather hear about what's new in your life." Some people understood, and our relationships evolved. Others? Well, I never heard from them again, which told me everything I needed to know about why they really wanted to connect.

Chapter Six

Nurturing Meaningful Relationships

Choosing yourself, it's not just your life that changes—your relationships transform too. Each choice to live more authentically sent ripples through every relationship in my life. Some relationships evolved because others were on their own journeys of growth. Others shifted or ended because my choice to prioritize my well-being didn't fit their vision of who I should be. It's liberating and painful all at once, like watching a garden change seasons—some plants thrive while others fade away.

The Pain of Changing Relationships

When you start choosing yourself, you quickly discover that not everyone is ready for your transformation. It's like you're reading a different chapter of life than they are, and suddenly, the story doesn't sync up anymore.

I remember the first few months after leaving my corporate role. Certain colleagues—people I'd shared daily coffee runs and life updates with for years—just... disappeared. No dramatic falling out, no confrontation. Just silence. The kind of silence that speaks volumes. At first, I made excuses for it: "They're busy," "The holidays are coming up," "They probably don't know what to say." But as weeks turned into months, I had to face a harder truth: sometimes people leave not because you've done something wrong, but because your growth makes them uncomfortable.

It shows up in unexpected ways. Maybe you're scrolling through social media and see photos of a gathering you weren't invited to. Or you hear through the grapevine that former colleagues are meeting for happy hour—the same happy hour you used to organize. The exclusion stings, but what hurts more is realizing these relationships might have been built on circumstance rather than genuine connection.

The hardest part? The questions that keep you up at night: Did these relationships mean as much to them as they did to me? Were we ever really friends or just convenient allies in the corporate world? Did I do something wrong? The lack of closure can feel like a wound that won't quite heal.

When Relationships Disappear

Think about ghosting in dating—how someone just vanishes without explanation. Now, imagine that happening with multiple relationships at once. That's what it feels like when you make a major life change, like leaving a long-term career. These were people I had lunch with, shared inside jokes with, and traveled with. For 30 years, they were part of my world. I was ready for my routine to shift, but I wasn't prepared for the silence that followed.

You expect some changes—fewer meeting invites and less day-to-day interaction. But what catches you off guard is how quickly some relationships fade to black. One day, you're exchanging daily texts and emoji reactions to workplace drama, but the next day, nothing. Your messages go unanswered. Your coffee invitations get declined or ignored. Your social media comments receive radio silence in return.

Maintaining Boundaries While Growing Forward

One of the trickiest parts of this journey has been navigating relationships with former colleagues who have stayed in touch. These aren't just professional connections—they're people with whom I've shared significant parts of my life. The challenge becomes: how do you honor those shared experiences while protecting new boundaries?

I learned this the hard way as conversations would quickly turn into venting sessions or company gossip. What started as casual catch-ups would spiral into hour-long download sessions about workplace drama. Every conversation seemed to circle back to who said what in which meeting or the latest political power play. My body's reaction was immediate—tension in my jaw, racing heart, and that night, I'd have nightmares about being back at work. It was always a clear signal that I needed to establish new boundaries to protect my peace.

I developed what I call my "Three C's" approach:

- Clear: Be upfront about what you can and can't discuss

- Consistent: Don't make exceptions that blur your boundaries

- Compassionate: Remember they're still in the environment you left

Here's what this looks like in practice:

- When former colleagues reach out to vent about work situations, I gently redirect: "I hear how frustrated you are. Rather than focus on what's wrong, what would you like to be different?"

- If someone starts sharing office gossip, I kindly but firmly say, "I've worked hard to create distance from that environment for my own wellbeing. Can we talk about what's going on in your life instead?"

- When invited to events where I know the conversation will center around workplace drama, I either decline or set clear time limits for my attendance.

The beauty of these boundaries? They've actually deepened some of these relationships. When we redirect conversations away from work drama to what's really going on in our lives, we often discover connections we never knew existed. Some of my strongest friendships now are with former colleagues—but they're based on who we are, not where we work.

The Duality of Grief and Growth

Here's what's fascinating about relationship transitions: grief and growth dance together in the most unexpected ways. You might be celebrating a new friendship that finally feels authentic while simultaneously mourning the loss of a decades-long work relationship. Both feelings are valid. Both deserve space.

I noticed this duality most clearly during my first few months after leaving corporate life. While I was grieving the loss of daily interactions with long-term colleagues, I was also discovering the joy of authentic connections through communities like Chief and Entreprenista. It was like watching a sunrise and sunset at the same time—one chapter closing as another opens.

The grief shows up in surprising moments:

- When Facebook memories pop up showing happy hours with former colleagues

- During holidays when traditions you used to share suddenly stop

- When you drive past your old office and muscle memory wants to turn in

- When you achieve something exciting and instinctively reach for your phone to text someone who's no longer in your life

But alongside that grief, growth appears just as unexpectedly:

- In the freedom to be fully yourself in new relationships

- Through connections based on genuine interest rather than corporate convenience

- In the discovery that some relationships actually deepen when you choose yourself

- Through the joy of attracting people who celebrate your authentic self

From Networking to Real Community

Picture this: You're at a networking event, clutching a stack of business cards, watching everyone else do the same awkward dance—trying to figure out who in the room might be "useful" to know. If you're anything like me, you're probably also calculating how soon you can leave without seeming rude.

Now, picture this instead: It's Friday morning, and you're joining an online co-working session. One by one, faces pop up on your screen: entrepreneurs, leaders, creators. Someone shares they're struggling with pricing their services. Immediately, three people offer to hop on a call to share their experiences. Another person drops helpful resources in the chat. No one's keeping score. No one's expecting anything in return. This is what a real community looks like.

This contrast between traditional networking and authentic community perfectly captures my own journey of transformation. It wasn't just about changing how I connected with others—it was about fundamentally changing how I showed up in relationships altogether.

I always thought of networking as something icky. My frame of reference was within the walls of a large organization, where networking was all about knowing the right person to help you get ahead. As a younger employee, it was pressure-filled—say the right thing, do the right thing, meet the right person, and your career was set. Honestly, it didn't even seem to matter if you were good at your job or deserved the promotion. If you knew the right person, that's all it took.

Later in my career, when I was in an executive role, I could spot these behaviors from a mile away. They called it networking; I called it butt-kissing. It never felt good, and I often felt used. Because of that, whenever I heard the words "networking" or "building relationships," I wanted to run. This was just another way the corporate world asked us to be inauthentic, to play a role rather than be ourselves.

Just when I was ready to swear off professional connections and networking entirely, I discovered communities that would completely change my understanding of what meaningful relationships could look like in the professional world.

The Chief Connection

Chief is a private network designed for senior women executives—the kind of women who've spent their careers being "the only one in the room." When I first joined, I was skeptical. After thirty years in corporate America, watching supposedly supportive networks turn into political battlegrounds, I had my guard up. Would this be just another place where women competed instead of connected?

What I found instead brought me to tears—in the best possible way. Here were women who understood what it meant to navigate male-dominated corporate cultures. They knew what it felt like to be told to "tone it down" or "be less intimidating." When someone shared a story about being the only woman in a boardroom, heads nodded in recognition. When another mentioned the delicate balance of being assertive without being labeled "aggressive," knowing looks were exchanged. It was like finding a room full of people who spoke a language I'd been speaking alone for years.

Over the past year, my Chief meetings have become almost like looking in a mirror—but one that reflects both backward and forward. I see my past self in the women still navigating corporate politics, wondering if there's more to life than climbing the ladder. I see my present self in those making bold transitions, choosing authenticity over advancement. And I see my future self in those who've already blazed trails beyond traditional corporate paths.

What is the difference between these connections and my old corporate relationships? There's no pretense. No political maneuvering. No need to maintain an image or guard your territory. Just real women supporting each other through real challenges and celebrations.

The Entreprenista Effect

But it was joining Entreprenista—a community specifically for women entrepreneurs—that showed me what was possible beyond corporate life entirely. If Chief helped me understand my past, Entreprenista opened my eyes to an entirely new future.

This isn't your typical business network; it's a vibrant community of women who are building their own paths, often after leaving successful corporate careers like mine. The energy here is completely different from anything I experienced in thirty years of corporate life.

These women understand something most people don't—the emotional rollercoaster of building your own path. On Monday, you're excited and optimistic about new possibilities. By Tuesday, you're convinced it's never going to work, and somehow, by Thursday, you're on top of the world with new leads or clients. Sound exhausting? It is. But here's the beautiful part: everyone in this community gets it.

What amazes me most is how these women support each other. Remember all those corporate "networking" events where everyone guarded their contacts and opportunities like dragons protecting treasure? This is the opposite. These women actively share resources, make introductions, and celebrate each other's successes—even when they're in similar businesses. The first time someone I barely knew offered to introduce me to three potential clients, I almost fell out of my chair. Where was the catch? What would she want in return?

The Power of Real Support

Turns out, there was no catch. Just women supporting women because they genuinely want to see each other succeed. It's been mind-blowing to experience what professional relationships can look like when you remove the corporate armor and competitive mindset.

The contrast between these new communities and my old corporate relationships has taught me something profound about support. In the corporate world, support often comes with strings attached: political alliances, future favors, and strategic advantages. But here, support flows freely, driven by a genuine desire to see others succeed.

Let me give you an example. Recently, I was struggling with pricing for my coaching services. In my corporate life, this would have been a closely guarded secret—something to figure out alone or risk appearing weak. Instead, I posted about it in the Entreprenista community. Within hours, I had:

- Three women offering to jump on calls to share their pricing strategies

- Two introductions to other coaches who'd navigated similar challenges

- Multiple people sharing their own pricing stories

- And even a few potential clients who appreciated my transparency

This kind of support isn't just about practical help—it's healing. It's showing me what's possible when we stop competing and start connecting. It's teaching me that the loss of those old relationships, while painful, made space for connections that align more deeply with who I am and who I'm becoming.

Building Authentic Connections

The shift from collecting business cards to building real community started with a question: What if connection, not networking, was the goal?

This sparked what I now call my Friday Ritual. I call them Virtual Diet Cokes, 20-minute get-to-know-you sessions where you bring your favorite drink (Diet Coke is not required, though it's my personal fuel of choice). Every Friday, I send out ten invites to people I've never met but who catch my eye across various online spaces. Think of it as intentional friend-dating for your professional life.

I look for people who:

- Give off that "my kind of human" vibe in their online presence

- Are doing work that makes me think, "Okay, that's cool"

- Could either add to or benefit from my wonderfully random network

- Share that "former corporate life" DNA

Yes, some weeks, it feels vulnerable to reach out. That old corporate voice inside my mind says, "What if they say no? What if they think you're selling something?" But I've learned that authentic connection is worth the risk of rejection.

When I connect with someone, I always start with these three questions that consistently create openings for real conversation:

1. "What lights you up about your work?" Instead of the standard "What do you do?", this question invites people to share what really matters to them.

2. "What's your biggest challenge right now?" This creates space for vulnerability and real conversation.

3. "How can I support you?" This shifts the focus from what you might get from the connection to what you can give.

The Ripple Effect of Authentic Community

The nice thing about choosing authentic relationships is how it creates ripples far beyond your immediate circle. When you start showing up as your genuine self, you give others permission to do the same. I see this with my coaching clients—how one authentic conversation leads to another, how one brave boundary encourages others to set their own.

This ripple effect hit home recently when helping my niece and nephew launch their business. Instead of teaching them traditional networking scripts, we focused on sharing their genuine excitement about their project. The results? My retail contact offered them holiday store space, a connection shared their story (hello, multiple orders!), and they even landed a paid video gig with a youth entrepreneurship group—all because people responded to their authentic passion.

Through this experience, they're learning early what took me decades to figure out—that real success comes from genuine connections, not strategic networking. Watching them navigate these opportunities with pure enthusiasm and authenticity, without the corporate armor I wore for so long, has been incredible.

Aha! Moment

The moment that changed everything for me came during a networking event shortly after leaving my corporate role. Someone asked me a simple but profound question: "Are you building relationships or just collecting business cards?"

I felt that question in my gut. For years, I'd approached networking as a numbers game—how many connections could I make, how many business cards could I collect, how many LinkedIn contacts could I add? But standing there, without my corporate title to hide behind, I realized something powerful: One authentic connection is worth more than a thousand unauthentic ones.

That's when I understood that transforming my approach to relationships wasn't just about building a network—it was about creating a community of genuine support. It was about moving from collecting business cards to cultivating real connections. Most importantly, it was about being the kind of person I needed when I was going through my own transitions.

Chapter Seven

When "Work Family" Isn't Family

Do you know what's harder than leaving a toxic relationship? Realizing you're in one. Especially when that relationship is with a company you've loved your entire life, one that's been part of your family story for generations, one that claims "we're family" while slowly making you question your own reality.

When Family Means Control

"We're like a family here!"

Those words echo differently now. But for thirty years, I didn't just believe them—I preached them. I defended this "family" against critics, championed its values, and celebrated its successes as my own. After all, this wasn't just any company—it was woven into the fabric of my childhood. My dad had worked there. I'd grown up attending their holiday parties, summer camps, and family events. This was home.

Until it wasn't.

When Truth Can No Longer Be Ignored

Remember those whispers we talked about earlier? The ones telling you to choose yourself? Well, they got louder with each strained relationship, each moment of questioning who I could trust. By the time I found myself in that secret meeting with senior leadership—arranged at an odd hour in a room I didn't even know existed—those whispers had become a roar.

The leader across the table knew why I was there before I said a word. They knew about the toxic environment from neighborhood party gossip. They knew meeting with me would likely end my career there. And somehow, that all seemed normal. That meeting wasn't just about sharing problems—it was the moment I realized I'd have to let go of everything I thought I knew about this "family" to move forward.

Think about that for a minute. Senior leadership knows there's a serious problem, hears about it at neighborhood parties, and still needs employees to risk their careers to officially report it. That's not family—that's dysfunction wrapped in denial.

The Gaslighting Game

Those meetings with leadership weren't just wake-up calls about my career—they were devastating revelations about relationships I'd trusted my entire professional life. These weren't just random leaders; these were people who'd been instrumental in my rise to the executive level, who I'd worked alongside for three decades, and who regularly sought my insights about what was really happening in the organization.

I remember sitting in their office that Monday morning, my favorite drink in hand, having just spent the first few minutes chatting about holiday weekends: their kids, family gatherings, and the normal small talk that makes you feel connected to someone. The betrayal cut that much deeper when they shifted gears and acknowledged the toxic environment. They knew how bad it was, but instead of taking action, they wanted me to help hide it. These were the same people who had championed my career, who I had trusted completely, who just moments ago were sharing holiday stories with me, now asking me to prop up the dysfunction they claimed to want to fix.

"They are so coachable," they'd say "and they are trying so hard," they'd insist. "We need to help them be successful," they'd plead.

After these conversations, I'd walk away questioning myself. Maybe I was the problem? Maybe I needed to try harder? Then I'd look at the file of documented issues, of problems swept under the rug, of women being treated differently than men, and reality would come rushing back. But that's how gaslighting works—it makes you doubt your own perceptions, your own experiences, your own truth.

When Support Becomes Betrayal

The hardest part? Watching relationships I'd invested decades in revealing themselves as conditional. Those senior leaders who'd been my mentors? Silent when I needed them most.

One of the deepest cuts came from someone I worked closely with. We'd been in the trenches together, or so I thought. We shared the same struggles and supported each other through the chaos. People tried to plant doubts between us, and I chose to believe in our connection. Now, they don't speak to me at all. The truth of what happened there might always remain a mystery.

Another senior leader who had once been a daily presence in my life, who sought my counsel and trusted my judgment, never talked to me again except to criticize me after I spoke up. Others received expensive gifts and gift cards for the holidays from them. I didn't even get a Christmas card. The message was clear: family love was conditional on compliance.

Daily, after I resigned, I could see these same colleagues viewing my LinkedIn profile. No messages, no connection requests—just silently watching, like glimpsing familiar faces through a window but never being invited in.

What stung most was watching this play out with people I'd personally mentored, promoted, and considered friends. People whose careers I'd championed, whose battles I'd fought, whose successes I'd celebrated. Once I made the decision to leave, they not only disappeared from my life but doubled down on publicly supporting the system they'd privately condemned.

The whole experience forced me to confront an uncomfortable truth: in many cases, what I'd thought were genuine relationships built on trust and mutual respect were actually alliances of convenience. Just like that moment when I finally said "I will choose myself" in my personal relationship years before, I felt the weight of every relationship I'd built over three decades shift and reshape itself in my mind. The "work family" I'd believed in for so long had shown its true colors, and there was no going back to seeing things the way I had before.

When Values Become Vapor

Do you know those inspirational quotes and values they paint on office walls? The ones in fancy fonts with beautiful photography behind them? I used to believe in them so completely that I'd defend them to anyone who questioned their authenticity. After all, they weren't just words—they were supposed to be our guiding principles.

But watching how leadership protected their friends instead of addressing documented problems, seeing how quickly "family" turned their backs when I spoke up, experiencing firsthand how retaliation worked... well, let's just say I learned to read between the lines.

Let me translate some corporate speak for you:

"We value relationships" really means "We value relationships with our friends or people who can help us climb the ladder."

"We encourage you to be yourself" actually means "Be yourself... until it makes us uncomfortable."

"We don't tolerate toxicity or discrimination" translates to "Unless addressing it means holding our buddies accountable."

"Retaliation is not tolerated" really means "Unless we're the ones retaliating so you will leave and we can go back to pretending everything's fine."

"We're family and don't walk away" means "Stay in line or watch how quickly family becomes strangers."

The hardest part wasn't learning this translation—it was accepting that I had once been fluent in speaking it myself.

The Pain of Letting Go

You'd think after all this, letting go would be easy. But here's what nobody tells you about leaving a toxic work environment—it's like leaving an abusive relationship. Even when you see the manipulation clearly, letting go of the good memories, the relationships you thought were real, the identity you built there is gut-wrenching.

I had to accept that either the company had changed, or I had changed, or most likely, we both had. The company moved from trusting employees to demanding metrics, from valuing people to valuing processes. Through years of centralization and efficiency drives, what was once the work of four people became the expectation for one. As for me, with age came wisdom, and with wisdom came the uncomfortable clarity that what I'd defended for so long wasn't what I'd believed it to be.

Making Space for Something New

Just like those earlier moments of choosing myself, this wasn't just about walking away. It was about creating space for something different, something more authentic. But first, I had to release my grip on what was familiar, even if what was familiar had become toxic.

The first step was removing myself from the gossip chain. No more venting sessions about leadership, no more complaint circles that felt supportive but kept me tethered to the toxicity. With each step back, each boundary set, each truth acknowledged, something shifted not just in how I saw the organization but in how I saw myself.

As I began to let go of the "work family" myth, I started to recognize what real support could look like. It didn't have to come with strings attached. It didn't require compromising your values. It didn't mean choosing between loyalty and truth.

Aha! Moment

It wasn't actually during that secret meeting with the senior leader that everything clicked. It was weeks later, as I sat at my kitchen table, finally allowing myself to imagine a life beyond these walls that had defined me for so long. I realized something profound: A truly healthy organization doesn't need secret rooms for truth-telling. A real family doesn't make you choose between loyalty and honesty. And sometimes, letting go isn't about becoming someone new—it's about remembering who you were before you learned to doubt yourself.

The scariest part wasn't the thought of leaving. It was the realization that staying meant continuing to compromise who I was becoming. Just like those earlier moments of choosing myself (moving to Disney, studying in England), this wasn't just about walking away. It was about making space for something new to emerge.

Looking Ahead

As I began to loosen my grip on the "work family" illusion, something unexpected happened. The energy I'd spent maintaining relationships built on conditional acceptance became available for building genuine connections. The mental space occupied by managing office politics cleared for dreaming up new possibilities.

What I didn't know then, but can see clearly now, is that letting go of false family wasn't just an ending—it was an opening. An opening to discover what real support feels like. An opening to build relationships based on genuine connection rather than corporate agendas. An opening to remember who I was before I learned to make myself smaller to fit someone else's definition of family.

Remember: Sometimes, letting go of what you thought you had is the only way to create space for what you truly need. Trust that voice inside you. It knows the way forward.

Chapter Eight

The Practice of Letting Go

Remember how I had to let go of not just my corporate job but my whole identity as an executive? How those relationships I thought were friendships turned out to be more about convenience than connection? Letting go isn't just about physical things; it's about releasing old stories, outdated definitions of success, and ways of being that no longer serve us.

Your Letting Go Practice

Before we dive into specific letting-go exercises, I want to note that many of these practices will be expanded upon in our Integration section (Chapters 12-15). Think of these as your starter tools—the essential practices you need right now to begin letting go.

Exercise 1: What's Ready for Release?

Time needed: 45 minutes, a quiet space, and maybe your favorite drink (you know mine's Diet Coke!)

Sometimes, we don't even realize what we're holding onto until we take a good look. Remember how I started with taking down photos in my office, then moved to unfriending people on social media, and finally had to face those deeper questions about who I really was beyond my executive role?

Let's figure out what you might be ready to release. Grab your journal, get comfy, and let's dig in:

First, let's do a quick check-in:

- What's been nagging at you lately? (You know, those things that keep you up at 3 AM.)
- Where do you feel yourself holding back?
- What relationships feel different these days?
- What parts of your life feel heavy?

Now, just like I had to be honest about those workplace "friendships" that turned out to be more about convenience than connection, let's get real about what's really going on:

For each thing you listed, ask yourself:

- Am I holding onto this out of habit, fear, or loyalty?

- What would feel lighter if I let this go?

- What might become possible if I created this space?

Here's the thing about letting go: your body usually knows before your mind does. Remember how I told you about my tension headaches and jaw clenching? Those were clues I ignored for way too long. So let's check in with your body:

- Where are you holding tension?

- What situations make your stomach knot up?

- When does your jaw clench?

- What conversations make you hold your breath?

Trust these signals; they're your inner wisdom speaking, just like mine was when I started clearing my office long before I consciously decided to leave.

Exercise 2: Your Essential Letting Go Toolkit

Time needed: 30 minutes

This is your starter toolkit for release. We'll build on these foundations with more comprehensive practices in Chapter 12: Possibilities Practice, but for now, let's focus on the essentials:

Physical Release:

- What tangible items are ready to go? (Like those corporate awards I finally took down.)

- What spaces need refreshing?
- What physical reminders are keeping you stuck?

Digital Release:

- What online connections need updating?
- Which digital spaces need boundaries?
- What virtual habits are holding you back?

Emotional Release:

- What stories are you ready to let go of?
- What expectations no longer fit?
- What emotions need acknowledgment before release?

Exercise 3: Building Real Connections

Time needed: However long it takes to get honest with yourself

Remember when I told you about my shift from those awkward networking events to my virtual Diet Coke chats and how different it felt to just be real with people instead of playing the corporate game? Let's create your own way of building genuine connections.

Start with getting clear on what you want:

- What kind of conversations energize you?

- Who do you find yourself wanting to learn from?

- What topics light you up?

- What boundaries do you need?

Here's what my template for reaching out looks like (feel free to make it your own!):

"Hi [Name], I noticed [something specific that caught your attention: a post they wrote, a comment they made, a shared experience]. I'm building genuine connections with people who inspire me, and I'd love to have a virtual coffee chat to learn more about [whatever interests you about their work/life/experience]. No agenda beyond real connection. Would you be open to a 15-minute conversation?"

I send ten of these invitations every Friday. Some people say yes, some say no, some don't respond at all—and that's okay! The goal isn't to collect contacts; it's to find your people.

Set a weekly goal for yourself and block time on your calendar! My advice is to also include a calendar link, like Calendly, as it makes scheduling these much easier.

Note: We'll expand on building authentic relationships and creating deeper connections in Chapter 15: The Practice of Integration, but these starter practices will help you begin creating meaningful connections right away.

Exercise 4: First Steps Forward

Time needed: 15 minutes

Choose ONE thing to release this week. Just one. Remember, this isn't a race. Here are some ideas:

- A photo or memento that carries heavy energy
- A social media connection that no longer serves you
- An obligation that drains rather than fills you
- A story you've been telling yourself that's ready to be released

Next Steps: Your Action Plan

Remember how I needed nine months after that executive meeting to make my move? Your timeline is your own. Here's how to start:

1. Pick ONE Thing to Release This Week

    - Choose something small but meaningful
    - Set a specific date and time to let it go
    - Decide exactly how you'll release it (donate, delete, shred, etc.)
    - Tell one trusted person about your plan

2. Create Your Release Ritual
   - Schedule 30 uninterrupted minutes
   - Choose a location that feels supportive
   - Bring anything that helps you feel grounded (journal, favorite drink, music)
   - Plan what you'll say or do to mark the moment

3. Document Your Journey
   - Notice how your body feels before and after
   - Write down what surprised you
   - Record what felt easier or harder than expected
   - Track any resistance that comes up

4. Celebrate Your Courage
   - Plan something specific to acknowledge your step
   - Maybe a favorite meal, a walk in nature, or time with a supportive friend
   - Share your achievement with someone who gets it
   - Take a moment to really feel proud of yourself

These are your starter tools. Like my gradual office clearing that started months before I resigned, each small release builds momentum. As you progress through this book, we'll build on these fundamentals with more comprehensive practices in the Integration section. For now, focus on creating space—we'll explore what to fill it with later.

Ready to discover what becomes possible once you create this space? The next section is all about dreaming bigger and designing what's next—just like I had to imagine a life beyond those corporate walls that had defined me for so long.

Visit www.kristenchimack.com for digital resources and to subscribe to the Kickin' it with Kristen newsletter

Part 3
Possibilities

"Remember when anything seemed possible? That feeling doesn't disappear with age; it just gets buried under 'shoulds' and expectations. Sometimes the best opportunities appear right after you stop forcing life to fit your carefully crafted plans."

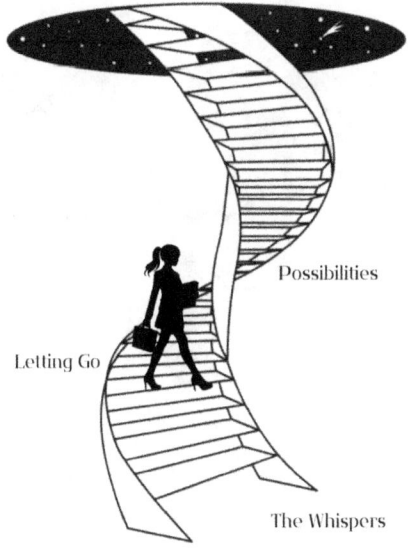

Growth Through Grief Spiral

Chapter Nine

Redefining Success

Success is a funny thing. The image we grow up with—a great career, marriage, 2.5 kids, white picket fence—is like this one-size-fits-all template for happiness. But life has a way of teaching you that success looks different for everyone, and more importantly, it can look different for *you* at different stages of your life.

Rewriting the Rules of Personal Success

When Traditional Paths Don't Fit

"You would make such an amazing mom, and we all want you to have that chance."

The words hung in the air, heavy with good intentions. A well-meaning family member expressed what everyone seemed to think. I knew they meant well, but in that moment, something crystallized for me. Yes, I wanted to be a mom, too—but not at the cost of rushing into the wrong relationship just to check that box. That 10-year relationship I stayed in, hoping things would change, was time I couldn't get back. But what were people expecting—for me to snap my fingers, manifest the perfect relationship, and instantly have a baby?

I remember sitting at family gatherings, watching my siblings with their kids, feeling that mix of joy and sadness. Everyone's path seemed so clear, so traditional—meet someone in your twenties, get married, have kids, and live happily ever after. Meanwhile, there I was, approaching forty, single again after ending that long-term relationship and completely off the "normal" timeline.

The questions were relentless:

- "Don't you want kids before it's too late?"
- "Aren't you worried about being alone?"
- "Maybe you're just too picky?"

Each one felt like a tiny judgment about my version of success being somehow less valid than theirs.

Finding Your Own Way

Sometimes, the path to redefining success starts with letting go of what you thought you wanted, or rather, how you thought you'd get it. For me, that meant embracing a different kind of motherhood. Instead of having my own kids, I poured my love and energy into being the best aunt I could be. And guess what?

The universe has a funny way of giving you what you need, just packaged differently than you expected.

Let me tell you about my special "5-year-old trips." When each of my nieces and nephews turns five, they get to pick anywhere in the US they want to go—just them and Aunt Kristen. My family thought I was crazy when I started this tradition. "You're going to take a 5-year-old across the country? By yourself?" But these trips have become something magical.

There was the time my nephew chose Disney World (of course!) and declared me the "best aunt ever" because I rode Space Mountain with him six times in a row. Or when my niece picked New York City, and we spent an entire afternoon in the American Girl store, creating stories for her doll. Or the texts from my nephew in college, saying he just found pictures from his 5-year-old trip when cleaning out his closet, and how many great memories he had of the time we spent in Washington, D.C. These moments—they're different from being a mom, sure, but they're no less meaningful.

Today, I wouldn't trade my relationships with my nieces and nephews for anything. From those special trips to arcade adventures (we're slightly obsessed with claw machines), from bowling days to simple dinners—I get to be fully present in their lives. They want me at their games and competitions. They look for me afterward. They call for advice. Had I had my own kids, I know these relationships would have been different and probably not as close. Sometimes, what feels like a "failed" traditional path leads you to something even better.

Lessons from Blended Family Life

But just when I thought I had this new definition of success figured out, life threw me another curveball—becoming a stepmom. Talk about redefining success! I came into my stepkids' lives when they were teenagers, carrying all these expectations about what our relationship would look like. Let me tell you, reality had other plans.

In my head, I had this perfect vision of blended family life. We'd have these amazing family dinners where everyone shared stories about their day. We'd plan fun weekend activities together. We'd bond over inside jokes and create new family traditions. All those things you see in heartwarming movies about blended families.

The reality was more like trying to choreograph a dance where everyone was listening to different music. Something as simple as birthdays taught me a profound lesson about adjusting expectations.

In the first half of my marriage, my birthdays would come and go without a word from my stepkids—not even a text. It hurt. In my family, birthdays were these big, important celebrations. I remember planning this elaborate day for their dad's birthday, imagining us all hanging out, talking, and playing games. Reality? They showed up, ate, and left. I felt like they couldn't wait to get out of there.

But here's where redefining success really hit home. One day, I was complaining to my friend about how quickly they left after dinner, and she asked me something that changed my perspective: "But they came, right?" She was right. They showed up. In their world, with their experiences and background, showing up WAS the win. I had been so focused on what success should look like (long, intimate family gatherings) that I missed what success actually looked like (them choosing to be there at all).

Over time, I've learned that choosing myself in this relationship sometimes means letting go of expectations that could lead to disappointment or hurt. Success isn't about achieving some picture-perfect blended family ideal; it's about accepting that my stepkids might want a different kind of relationship than I initially hoped for. Each year, I measure success simply by whether our relationship stays steady or grows stronger, even if that growth looks different than I imagined. The win isn't in grand gestures or perfect family moments but in the small signs that we're all choosing to be part of each other's lives in whatever way feels authentic to each of us.

The Evolution of Professional Success

Just as my personal definition of success shifted, my professional viewpoint underwent its own transformation. That executive meeting we've been talking about wasn't just about leaving a dysfunctional situation; it was about completely reimagining what career success meant to me.

The First Whispers of Change

I had always planned to work until 65, but something began to stir inside me in my mid-40s. That familiar voice that had guided me to choose myself before—in leaving for Disney, in studying abroad, in ending that relationship—was back. There had to be more to life than climbing the corporate ladder, right?

The first hint came during a routine Tuesday morning meeting. I was sitting there, watching everyone nod along to something we all knew wasn't going to work, and I had this sudden thought: "Is this really what success looks like? Pretending to agree with things we know are wrong?"

Breaking Free from Traditional Metrics

The metrics I'd used for years—promotions, titles, paychecks—suddenly felt hollow. I started questioning everything:

- Was success really about having an impressive title if it meant being complicit in a toxic environment?

- Did success mean sacrificing my authenticity for a bigger paycheck?

- Was staying until retirement really "winning" if it cost me my peace of mind?

I remember the exact moment this hit home. I was in my office, looking at all the awards and certificates on my wall—the tangible proof of my "success"—and I felt nothing. Actually, worse than nothing. I felt trapped. Here I was, at the peak of what traditional success looked like, and I was miserable.

The Moment of Clarity

But sometimes, it takes a crisis to really see how far your definition of success has drifted from what truly matters. For me, that clarity came during COVID. Picture this: We'd just sent the entire company home for safety, but I was required to work in what they called the "crisis war room." Up to ten of us crammed into close quarters for weeks, working 12+ hour days. When we were finally allowed to work from home, one of the executives required us to stay on live conference calls from early morning until sometimes midnight.

I can still hear my husband yelling up the stairs, "Your computer's talking!" as I'd run back down from a quick bathroom break, only to find out someone needed a simple formatting change on a document. It was worse than being on call—it was like being under surveillance.

That crisis room experience crystallized everything—this wasn't success. This wasn't even rational. This was madness dressed up as dedication. And suddenly, redefining professional success wasn't just an intellectual exercise—it was a survival necessity.

Pay attention to the signs that your current definition of success might not be serving you:

- When achievements feel hollow (like that executive position that filled me with dread instead of pride)

- When explaining your choices becomes exhausting (like those years of defending why I valued my nieces' and nephews' events over late-night work demands)

- When your body is screaming "enough" (like during COVID, running up and down stairs for midnight PDF emergencies)

- When you catch yourself saying, "I should be happy, but..." (like having everything society says you should want—title, salary, status—but feeling completely disconnected from your values)

Our bodies are way ahead of our minds when it comes to recognizing misaligned success. While I was still weighing the practical implications of leaving—the steady paycheck, the benefits, the career trajectory—my body had already made its decision. The headaches, the anxiety, the constant tension; these weren't just stress symptoms. They were my inner wisdom screaming, "Enough!"

Understanding this changed everything. I realized I didn't need anyone else's permission to define success differently. I didn't need to explain why peace of mind was worth more than a pension or why being fully present for my family mattered more than a prestigious title.

Of course, the voices in my head tried to keep me in line: "But what about your six-digit salary? The bonus? The benefits? No one leaves before their pension kicks in." Those voices were loud, and they had a point. But here's what I've learned about success: Sometimes, the greatest success lies in having the courage to walk away from what everyone else thinks you should want.

Creating a New Vision

When I finally decided to leave, I was laser-focused on making sure whatever came next aligned perfectly with my core values, passions, and allowed me to be 100% authentically me. After all those years of compromise, I wanted to wake up excited and energized about what the day held. I was done with working to live—I wanted to live to work. Most importantly, I wanted to surround myself with positive, uplifting, and inspiring people.

The road I took wasn't a straight line. It never is when you're rewriting the rules of success. Within a few weeks of leaving corporate life, I had created a company, developed a strategy, and opened my doors as a leadership coach. Things happened fast. I quickly had coaching clients, was invited on a podcast, launched an online course, and started a weekly newsletter. From the outside, it looked like everything was falling perfectly into place.

But you know that voice I've mentioned? The one that had pushed me to choose myself so many times before? Well, it was back, whispering that familiar message: "There has to be more..."

This time, though, I recognized it immediately. Instead of ignoring it or pushing it aside, I went to work, trying to figure out what was missing. I talked to people in my network, made lists of what I loved about my past roles, what I missed about my corporate career, and what truly ignited my passions.

After several months of exploration, it hit me: I missed traveling, I missed working with people to solve challenges, and I missed working on events—one of the roles I'd loved most in my corporate career. Just like that moment in the executive's office had shown me what I needed to leave behind, this realization showed me what I needed to move toward.

So, after six months of coaching, I decided to pivot. Not abandon what I'd built, but expand it to better align with my passions. I started working as a hotel sourcer, helping others—both individuals and companies—find, source, and contract hotels for their events. Now, I spend my time combining both worlds: coaching others to live their most authentic lives through retreats AND helping others plan their events.

The New Definition of Success

These days, success looks radically different:

- Freedom to choose my work
- Ability to be present for family moments
- Making a genuine impact
- Finding joy in what I do
- Creating meaningful experiences for others

My mornings start with a Diet Coke run—a small ritual that brings me joy. I start work around 9 AM (unless I choose not to), enjoy lunch with my husband, and spend my days in a mix of activities I love:

- Helping clients find perfect venues for their events

- Coaching leaders through their transitions

- Meeting new people through virtual and in-person networking sessions

- Traveling to exciting destinations for retreats and events

The challenging days look different now, too. Instead of being drained by office politics and harmful dynamics, I'm energized by the "good" kind of challenges—the ones that come from growth and success. When a contract negotiation gets complicated or a client needs extra support, it feels purposeful rather than political. These challenges push me to grow rather than shrink myself to fit someone else's expectations.

At first, these changes felt separate—redefining personal success as an aunt and stepmom and reimagining professional success beyond the corporate ladder. But gradually, like pieces of a puzzle finding their way together, I began to see how these "separate" definitions of success were actually creating one authentic whole.

Writing Your Success Story

Do you know those permission slips we needed for school field trips? The ones that gave us official approval to step away from the normal routine and try something new? Well, I've realized that as adults, we're still waiting for permission slips—except now we're waiting for someone else to tell us it's okay to define success differently.

Here's the thing: We don't need to wait. We can write our own permission slips. But this isn't just about scribbling down a quick note; it's about really understanding what we're giving ourselves permission to do, acknowledging both the doubts we'll face (from ourselves and others), and embracing the truth we need to hear.

Here were the permission slips I had written for my journey.

Permission to Define Success Differently

What it means:

Looking at success through your own lens, not society's expectations. For me, it meant walking away from an executive role I'd worked 30 years to achieve—leaving not just a job but an entire identity I'd built. It meant embracing being an aunt to 11 amazing kids instead of pursuing traditional motherhood. It meant accepting that my relationship with my stepkids might never look like the blended family stories you see in movies or even ones that my friends have built with their stepkids.

The External Voices:

- "How can you walk away from all that security?"
- "You're giving up everything you worked for!"
- "But you'd be such a great mom; don't you want your own kids?"
- "Surely you can stick it out a few more years for the pension?"
- "What will people think if you leave at the peak of your career?"

The Internal Doubts:

- Will I regret leaving before my pension kicks in?
- What if I'm making a massive mistake walking away from corporate life?
- Should I have tried harder to have my own kids?
- Am I failing as a stepmom because our relationship doesn't look like I imagined?
- What if I never find something as "prestigious" as my executive role?

The truth I need to hear:

Those years aren't wasted—they're preparation. Every role, every experience, every supposed "wrong" turn is actually building your unique path. Just like my moves from Finance to HR to Events weren't scattered, it was gathering the exact skills I'd need for my future. And those relationships that don't fit the traditional mold? They're exactly what they need to be.

Permission to Change Your Mind

What it means:

Allowing yourself to pivot when something's not working. For me, this meant leaving that corporate role I'd dedicated three decades to. It meant starting a coaching business and then having the courage to admit I missed event planning. Instead of forcing myself to stick with just one path, I gave myself permission to combine both passions.

The External Voices:

- "But you just left your stable career for this!"
- "Shouldn't you pick one thing and stick with it?"
- "Are you sure you want to start over again?"
- "Why can't you just be content with what you have?"

The Internal Doubts:

- Am I just running away when things get hard?
- What if I keep changing my mind and never find my path?
- Will anyone take me seriously if I keep pivoting?
- Maybe I should have stayed in my corporate role?

The truth I need to hear:

Change isn't failure—it's growth. Every time you honor that inner voice telling you, "There's more," you're not being fickle; you're being faithful to your authentic self. Sometimes, the bravest thing you can do is admit that what worked before isn't working now.

Permission to Count Different Wins

What it means:

Celebrating the victories that matter to you, even if others don't understand; choosing peace of mind over a pension; celebrating when my stepkids simply show up instead of expecting picture-perfect family moments; finding joy in being the aunt who creates special memories rather than trying to force myself into a traditional mom role.

The External Voices:

- "But what about your retirement?"
- "You're walking away from all that status!"
- "Aren't you worried about your future?"
- "Don't you want more from your family relationships?"

The Internal Doubts:

- Can I really build something meaningful on my own?
- What if I regret not staying for my full pension?
- Am I settling for less in my relationships?
- Should I have pushed harder for traditional success?

The truth I need to hear:

There are costs to choosing differently—your bank account might take a hit, relationships might shift, and people might question you. But there are also gains that don't show up on any balance sheet:

- Peace of mind (goodbye Sunday night dread!)
- Energy (it's amazing how much vitality returns when you're not drowning in toxicity)

- Joy (the kind that makes you excited to start each day)
- Freedom (to create, choose, and simply be)

The beautiful thing about redefining success is how it ripples through every part of your life. When you release the need to compartmentalize, something amazing happens: authenticity flows naturally between personal and professional spaces. Now, success means showing up fully as myself, whether I'm negotiating hotel contracts in my favorite hoodie or leading a coaching session.

Success isn't about checking boxes anymore—it's about creating a life that feels true to who you are, even if that life looks nothing like what you originally planned.

Aha! Moment

I was running up the stairs after another late-night emergency text about a PowerPoint that needed formatting, and suddenly, I started laughing. Not because it was funny but because everything became crystal clear.

Here I was, at the peak of what society defined as success—executive title, great salary, nice office—and I was running up and down stairs at midnight to change font sizes in a document.

I sat down on those stairs and asked myself: "If this is success, why does it feel like failure?"

That's when it hit me. I had spent years calculating the cost of leaving—the pension, the salary, the benefits, the status. But I had never calculated the cost of staying—my authenticity, my peace of mind, my joy, my health, precious moments with family that I'd never get back.

In that moment, sitting on those stairs at midnight, I made a decision: I would rather work at McDonald's and be true to myself than keep climbing a ladder that was leaning against the wrong wall. Sometimes, the biggest successes come disguised as moments of choosing yourself over everyone else's definition of success.

Chapter Ten

The Reality of Authentic Leadership

Do you know that moment in every superhero origin story when they realize their greatest challenge actually became their superpower? Well, grab your favorite drink and settle in because I'm about to share how choosing authentic leadership (and all the resistance that came with it) became my most powerful teacher.

Remember those earlier moments when choosing yourself felt terrifying? Choosing to lead authentically requires that same courage—releasing our grip on who we think we should be to become who we really are.

The Leadership Truth Document

I remember sitting in my office, staring at what I called my Leadership Truth Document, wondering if I was about to make the biggest mistake of my executive career. Nine hundred people across the United States were about to see who I was as a leader—no corporate speak, no carefully crafted image, just real expectations and promises I'd have to live up to every single day.

This wasn't just another glossy leadership philosophy statement filled with buzzwords like "servant leadership" and "open-door policy." (Seriously, has anyone's door ever actually been closed?) This was different. This was me, putting in writing exactly who I was as a leader—good days, bad days, and everything in between.

My hands would shake a little each time I started presenting it. "I believe in direct, honest communication," I'd tell them, "even when it's uncomfortable. You'll never have to guess where you stand with me or decode corporate speak to understand what I'm saying."

Then I'd share something that made their eyes widen: "On my best days, you'll find me energetic, creative, and ready to tackle anything. On my harder days (and yes, I have them), I might be quieter, a bit shorter with my words, or need more processing time. I'll always let you know which kind of day it is, and I invite you to do the same."

The room would usually go silent at this point. In a corporate culture where leaders were expected to be consistently "on," always polished, admitting to having off days felt radical. But then something magical would happen. Someone would sigh with relief. Another would lean forward, suddenly engaged. By the time I got to my non-negotiables—no throwing team members under the bus, no politics over performance, no pretending everything's fine when it isn't—people were actually taking notes.

"We've never had a leader talk to us like this," one team member told me after a meeting. "Usually, they just tell us their door is always open, and they move on." Another asked if they could create their own version for their team. What started as my terrifying experiment in authenticity was becoming something bigger.

While the Leadership Truth Document helped me define who I wanted to be as a leader, my journey also taught me powerful lessons about who I didn't want to be. Every frustrating experience, every moment of dysfunction, every example of poor leadership—they all became teachers, showing me what to avoid in my own leadership practice.

The Anti-Leadership Playbook: What Not to Do

Let me share some of the most powerful lessons I learned from bad bosses. Think of this as your "What Would My Bad Boss Do?" guide—and then do the opposite. These weren't just frustrating experiences; they were whispers trying to show me a different way to lead.

1. **Make Employees Coach Their Boss**

   Remember that meeting where I was asked to "coach" a struggling boss and prop up dysfunction? That wasn't just a bad day; it was my body telling me something was fundamentally wrong. Leadership flows down, not up. If you're ever asked to coach your own boss, see it as the red flag it is.

2. **Push the "We're Like a Family" Narrative**

   Bad bosses love saying, "We're like a family." It is code for: "We expect unconditional loyalty while giving conditional support." Think about it: would you expect your family to work until midnight? Miss important life events? Accept below-market pay because of "loyalty"?

3. **Protect Friends Over Function**

   Remember how senior leadership had heard about our toxic environment through neighborhood gossip? That taught me a crucial lesson: bad bosses always protect their friends instead of the company and employees. They will ignore documented problems because addressing them might upset their buddy in leadership.

4. **Ignore Disconnection**

   Let me tell you about Jake (not his real name). He was one of our top performers—until he wasn't. The change was subtle at first. Fewer contributions in meetings. Shorter email responses. Less engagement in team activities. By the time his leader noticed, he had one foot out the door. Bad bosses miss these warning signs until it's too late.

5. Question Legitimate Development

As a leader, I was told to develop employees and provide feedback. Yet when I met with two team members to discuss their career goals after a disappointing job decision, HR treated it like a major investigation. They questioned my motives and suggested I was intimidating employees, all because I did what leaders are supposed to do: help their people grow. Bad bosses make you afraid to actually lead.

6. Be a Request Relay Service

Picture this: It's midnight, I'm running up and down stairs because someone needs an urgent font change in a PowerPoint. Where was my boss? Not pushing back on this ridiculous request. Bad bosses just pass along every demand without protecting their team's time and energy.

7. Make Empty Promises

"We'll look into that." "Let me check on that." "I'll get back to you." Bad bosses turn these phrases into the corporate equivalent of "The check's in the mail." They dangle possibilities they never intend to deliver.

8. Say One Thing, Do Another

Bad bosses would acknowledge our toxic environment but expect us to keep working in it. They'd talk about work-life balance while sending midnight emails. Their actions rarely matched their words.

9. Fixate on Style Over Substance

Those late-night emergencies over font choices and slide layouts? Bad bosses care more about how things look than what they mean. They'll dismiss good work because they don't like the formatting.

10. Hire Only Carbon Copies

Remember that incredibly talented strategist I hired who didn't fit the traditional corporate mold? Bad bosses would have passed her by because she didn't fit their narrow definition of "cultural fit."

11. Make Support Conditional

In my corporate life, bad bosses always attached strings to their support: political alliances, future favors, strategic advantages. They saw support as currency to be traded, not given freely.

12. Share Performance Issues Behind Backs

> Bad Bosses will openly share their frustrations about others' poor performance while simultaneously telling you they will likely be promoted. Bad bosses talk about performance issues with everyone except the person who needs to hear it, creating confusion and destroying trust.

Remember that senior leadership meeting I mentioned earlier? The one where I learned they had heard about the horrible work environment at a neighborhood party? That moment wasn't just disappointing; it was a master class in the gap between talking about authentic leadership and actually practicing it.

I walked into that meeting carrying not just documentation and data but years of trust in our organization's values—the ones painted on our walls and repeated in every town hall. Family. Relationships. Doing the right thing. I truly believed that if I could just help them understand what was happening, they would take action. After all, they consistently spoke about the importance of our culture and how we took care of each other.

Instead, the casual admission that they had known about these issues for months and chosen to do nothing changed everything. It wasn't just disappointment I felt—it was betrayal. Here was the stark difference between talking about values and living them, between preaching authenticity and practicing it. Everyone talks about "bringing your whole self to work" until your whole self has something uncomfortable to say.

These leadership lessons weren't just theoretical; they were put to the test during a major PR crisis that showed what happens when authentic leadership collides with corporate politics.

When Truth Meets Politics

You know that feeling when you can sense something's off but can't quite put your finger on it? That's how it started. Information wasn't flowing right. Messages were getting twisted. People were having private conversations instead of speaking up in meetings. My body knew something was wrong before my mind could fully grasp it.

It took a public relations crisis to finally show me what those whispers had been trying to say. What started as a routine corporate challenge became the moment that would test everything I believed about authentic leadership and ultimately show me where that authenticity would lead.

It came to a head when an internal memo leaked to the media. In a traditional corporate response, everyone would circle the wagons, protect themselves, and stick to carefully crafted talking points. But I'd promised my team something different. I'd promised them truth, even when it was uncomfortable.

The finger-pointing started immediately: Who approved this? Who knew about it? How many people were involved? Every department seemed to have its own version of the truth, even though we had the real story right there in black and white on the approved proposal document.

But here's what really got me: people who had followed all the right processes and gotten all the proper approvals were suddenly feeling like they'd done something wrong because leaders wouldn't own their role in the process. Two public statements had to be retracted because people were afraid to tell their leaders the real story. Think about that; we were creating more problems trying to avoid the original one.

I had to let go of my instinct to figure out "who" was creating these challenges or trying to place blame. That wasn't serving anyone. Instead, I took a deep breath and made what felt like a radical choice: I called a senior leader directly.

"I need to be clear about something," I told her. "The information you've been given is inaccurate. This has led to two incorrect public statements, and we (the PR team) cannot do our job if people aren't willing to get in a room and talk about what really happened. We need to focus on getting to the truth so we can respond correctly."

This is where authentic leadership gets real. Some executives were in full self-protection mode, unwilling to engage in honest dialogue. But remember that Leadership Truth Document? The one where I promised my team I'd speak up for them and stand firm on ethical issues? This was the moment to live those words.

I gave my team permission to work around the resistant leaders and find creative ways to piece together the real story. It wasn't about throwing anyone under the bus; it was about finding a path to truth that would serve everyone better in the long run.

The Moment Everything Changed

As I drove home that night after the PR crisis, something shifted inside me. I'd spent the day doing what authentic leadership called for: seeking truth, protecting my team, refusing to play politics. And while we'd handled the situation well, the pushback I'd received for simply doing the right thing left me unsettled.

Sitting at a red light, I suddenly remembered something my grandma Gail used to say: "If you have to twist yourself into knots to fit somewhere, maybe you don't belong there." The truth hit me like a physical force. I was trying to be an authentic leader in an organization that didn't actually want authenticity. They wanted the appearance of authenticity, carefully managed and controlled, never threatening the status quo.

This wasn't just about navigating one more crisis or dealing with difficult personalities. This was about a fundamental misalignment between who I was becoming and what the organization needed me to be. The more I committed to leading authentically, the more obvious it became—I couldn't retire here. Not because it was a bad organization but because I had outgrown it.

That realization both terrified and liberated me. The carefully crafted retirement plan, the pension, the future I'd imagined—all of it would need to change. But for the first time in years, I felt something unexpected stirring beneath the fear: excitement about what might be possible if I stopped trying to fit where I no longer belonged.

When Truth Creates Tension

Leading authentically is like turning on a bright light in a room where everyone's gotten used to the dark. Some people blink and adjust. Others prefer the shadows. And once you start seeing clearly, you can't unsee what the light reveals.

Let me be honest about something that isn't covered in leadership books. The personal toll of trying to lead authentically in a resistant environment. It's not just about making tough decisions; it's about facing constant pushback against your very way of being.

I remember one particularly challenging day that perfectly captured this struggle. Let me share some real moments where choosing authenticity created tension and what they taught me about true leadership.

The Blog Incident

It started with a leader confronting me about my company blog. "You can't keep writing personal stories on your blog. It needs to be all business content," they declared.

There I was, sharing stories about game nights with my nieces and nephews, writing about the leadership lessons I learned from our claw machine adventures. "You can't keep writing personal stories," they insisted. "If you would stop talking about your family, my life would be easier."

They wanted authentic leadership, but only within carefully drawn lines. Be yourself, but not too much. Be real, but only in approved ways. Share personal stories, but make sure they're properly sanitized for corporate consumption.

The Development Meetings

That same day, I met with two employees who were disappointed because we had hired our summer intern for a position that they wanted to be considered for. Rather than letting their frustration fester, I sat down with each one to discuss their goals and development plans. It felt like the right thing to do, the authentic thing to do that aligned with my Leadership Truth Document.

But the next day, HR called. "Do you feel that talking to an employee about their goals and development was appropriate given you are their executive and there are leaders between you and them? Do you see that it probably felt intimidating?" Yet, the two employees thanked me and sent me emails saying how helpful it was to them.

The message was clear: maintain the hierarchy, stay in your lane, don't disrupt the system.

The Salary Increase

Before I could fully process that conversation, another call from HR came: "Did you give someone a salary increase to keep them from complaining about not being selected for a job in another area? We have heard you tried to buy them off."

I about fell out of my chair. Eight weeks earlier, long before any job decisions, I'd requested raises for a leader who I believed was being underpaid for their contributions. The fact that the news of their increase came the same day as the job decision was pure coincidence. When I explained this to HR, their response floored me: "Can you see how it could be interpreted as a payoff?"

"Maybe," I suggested, "we should be focused on why some think we need to pay people off and talk to those leaders?"

Even something as straightforward as giving a deserved raise became suspect. When HR suggested I was trying to "buy off" employees—when I'd requested those raises weeks before—I realized something profound. In a system built on politics and appearances, genuine actions are often seen as manipulative because that's what everyone's come to expect.

Each of these moments was like a crack in the foundation of what I believed about organizational leadership. The more I chose truth, chose authenticity, chose to live my values, the more these cracks spread. It wasn't just about isolated incidents anymore. It was about a fundamental misalignment between who I was becoming and what the organization needed me to be.

Creating Space for Others

The real power of authentic leadership isn't in what it costs you; it's in what it gives others. Let me share some stories that show what happens when you create an environment where people feel safe being real.

The Email Chain Incident

When one of my team members accidentally forwarded an entire email chain to a reporter instead of just the approved statement, something remarkable happened. Instead of panic or blame, they immediately took ownership, reached out to the reporter, and sent me an overview of what they had learned. My response? "Thank you for letting me know. Mistakes happen. I've done the exact same thing myself. You handled this perfectly."

That's what happens when people know they won't be punished for being human. They take ownership, learn from mistakes, and often handle situations better than if they were acting from fear.

The Unconventional Hire

I once fought to hire a high-level strategist who didn't fit our traditional mold: no college degree, visible tattoos, and a creative spirit that didn't quite match our buttoned-up culture. Other leaders worried about "fit." But they turned out to be one of the most talented people I've ever worked with. Why? Because authenticity isn't just about being real yourself; it's about creating space for others to be real, too.

Every authentic choice had been preparing me for this moment. From that first Leadership Truth Document to each small act of real connection, I'd been building the courage to face what I'd known deep down for a while: I had outgrown this place.

More importantly, I was beginning to glimpse something beyond the fear of leaving, a kind of joy I hadn't expected. What if all these tensions, all these moments of misalignment, weren't just pushing me away from something? What if they were also pulling me toward something else? Something that would allow me to be fully, completely myself?

That's when I remembered something else my grandma Gail used to say: "The truth might set you free, but first, it usually makes you really uncomfortable." She was right. The truth about authentic leadership had made me uncomfortable enough to finally see what I needed to do next. And somehow, in that discomfort, I found the first hints of real joy.

Making It Real

The real work of authentic leadership happens in daily moments. It's choosing truth over comfort, consistency over convenience, growth over stagnation. Here are practices that have helped me stay authentic even when it's hard:

The Morning Check-In

- How am I really feeling today?
- What truth needs to be spoken?

- Where might I be tempted to compromise?

The Decision Filter

- Does this align with my values?
- Am I choosing this for the right reasons?
- What would I advise someone else to do?

The Evening Reflection

- Where did I stay true to myself today?
- What could I have done differently?
- What did I learn about my leadership?

Aha! Moment

I was in a coaching session, sharing my frustration about all the leaders who hadn't spoken up about our environment, when my coach asked me a question that stopped me cold: "When did you stop speaking up?"

That's when it hit me. I had become part of the system I was criticizing. I thought back to all those private message chains complaining about incorrect information in meetings. During all those times, I looked the other way when I saw manipulative behavior, and during all those moments, I chose withdrawal over pushing back. I'd been telling myself I was being strategic, being supportive of others who were struggling, being smart about picking my battles.

But the truth was harder to face: I had stopped being authentic long before I left. I had played the game, participated in politics, and helped maintain the culture I claimed to want to change. Sometimes, the hardest part of authentic leadership isn't recognizing what others are doing wrong; it's acknowledging your own role in maintaining the status quo.

Looking Forward

That executive meeting wasn't just about an unhealthy work environment or a difficult boss. It was the moment I finally understood: I couldn't keep pretending. I couldn't be an authentic leader in an inauthentic system.

Each time I chose truth over pretense, direct communication over corporate speak, and real connection over political maneuvering, I felt lighter. More alive. More me. Leading authentically isn't just about being yourself; it's about discovering that being yourself is actually the way to joy.

And that joy? It starts showing up in unexpected moments:

- The relief of saying exactly what you think
- The energy after having honest conversations
- The peace that comes from stopping the pretense

- The freedom of leading from truth

Remember: Just like choosing yourself opened doors to personal growth, choosing authentic leadership creates possibilities you never imagined. Trust the process. Keep choosing truth. Your authentic leadership voice is waiting to emerge.

And yes, keeping a steady supply of your favorite drink nearby definitely helps. Trust me on this one.

Chapter Eleven

The Joy of Choosing You

Let me paint you a picture of joy: It's 9 AM, I'm in my favorite hoodie, hair in a messy bun, sipping my first Diet Coke of the morning. I've already had two incredibly productive client calls, and I'm about to hop on a virtual Diet Coke chat with someone I'm excited to connect with. No corporate mask, no political navigation, no pretense. Just me, being fully myself, doing work I love.

Picture that against my former life: It's 7 AM, I've already been at my desk for an hour, a tension headache brewing as I carefully craft messages to avoid ruffling feathers. Would today be the day someone caught me being too much, too direct, too authentic, too me? Would my direct communication style clash with their need for "strategic messaging"? Would I have to sit through another meeting nodding along to things I knew weren't true?

If you're wondering if choosing yourself is worth it, let me show you what's possible on the other side.

The Simple Joys

Sometimes, it shows up in the most mundane moments. Like that first morning, I realized I could take a Diet Coke run whenever I wanted. No sneaking out between meetings, no apologizing for taking a break, no rushing back for fear of missing an "emergency." Just a simple pleasure, enjoyed without guilt.

My days unfold naturally: no alarm clocks, no dress code (hello, yoga pants!), no Sunday night anxiety. Those tension headaches and stomach knots from corporate life? Gone. Instead, I've found what freedom feels like in my body: restful sleep, lasting energy, and even better posture. Turns out authenticity has great ergonomics.

Joy in Authentic Work

Here's the surprising truth about choosing yourself: work becomes energizing when you stop managing perceptions and start creating real value. Even stress feels different, it's the productive tension of growth rather than the drain of maintaining a façade.

Yes, I earn less now than I did as an executive, but I've gained something more valuable: peaceful sleep, genuine connections, and the freedom to be fully present. Success isn't measured in titles or salaries anymore but in lives touched, authentic relationships built, and the quiet satisfaction of ending each day as myself.

The Joy of Real Connection

Oh, the joy of authentic relationships! Instead of networking events where everyone is focused on selling themselves, I get to experience real community. My virtual Diet Coke chats have become my signature way of connecting, and guess what? Being completely myself—no makeup, comfy clothes, and all—has attracted more genuine connections than any polished networking strategy ever did.

Picture this: It's Friday morning, and I'm joining an Entreprenista Focus Friday co-working session. One by one, women pop into the virtual room, sharing what they're working on—no pretense, no hidden agendas. Just real entrepreneurs supporting each other.

During one recent session, I watched the chat light up with celebrations that would have seemed small in my corporate days but now represent real, meaningful wins:

- "Just finished a proposal for a client I'm excited to work with!"

- "Finally caught up on my expense tracking!"

- "Sent out ten networking requests!"

- "Created next month's social media content!"

What struck me wasn't just the wins themselves but the immediate response from the community. When someone mentioned researching social media tools, two different members shared their experiences with various platforms. No one was hoarding information or playing politics—just entrepreneurs helping entrepreneurs.

Navigating the New Uncertainty

Let me be real with you about entrepreneurial uncertainty. Yes, it exists, but it's a completely different flavor than what I experienced in corporate life. Back then, uncertainty meant wondering if my authentic self was "too much," if speaking truth would derail my career, or if the next reorganization would undo years of relationship building.

Now? When a deal falls through, or a lead ghosts me, it's just business. It is not personal, not political, but just part of the entrepreneurial journey. And here's what's wild: I actually handle these challenges better now than I ever did in corporate life.

Take last week, for example. I had three potential contracts stall out on the same day (because, apparently, the universe has a sense of humor). In my corporate days, this kind of setback would have sent me into a spiral of self-doubt and anxiety. Instead, I did something radical—I posted about it in one of my communities.

Within an hour, I had:

- Women sharing similar experiences and how they

bounced back

- Two potential new client referrals
- One offer to review my proposals and provide feedback
- And countless messages of support and encouragement

Compare that to the old days of suffering in silence or venting in endless reply-all emails that solved nothing. This new way of handling challenges isn't just more effective—it's more human.

Sure, some days, technology decides to have a personal vendetta against your virtual meetings. Some days, clients reschedule at the last minute. Some days, nothing seems to go according to plan. But here's the beautiful difference—I don't have to maintain some polished professional façade while dealing with these challenges. I can be real about the hard days, get the support I need, and trust that tomorrow will probably be better.

Plus, my coach helps me see opportunities I might miss while wallowing in temporary setbacks. And sometimes, the best solution is calling my girlfriends for an impromptu dinner out or convincing my husband it's time for another binge-watch of our favorite show. Let's be honest—sometimes, the most productive thing you can do is take a break and reset.

The Integration of Joy

Just like grief isn't a straight line, neither is joy. Some days, I still feel twinges of sadness about relationships lost or paths not taken. But now I understand—these feelings aren't opposites; they're partners in this dance of growth. Each moment of grief has led to unexpected joy, and each joy somehow helps heal old grief.

My greatest win? Today, I have zero negativity in my day. Think about that compared to before, when most of my day was full of people complaining about leadership, peers, direct reports, the company—everything. Every meeting and every discussion was laden with negative IMs about what was being said or the meeting after the meeting. It's shocking to think about how I survived in that environment for so long.

Today, I choose who I work with, when I work, and how I work—and I'm having fun! The negativity is gone, the passive-aggressive actions are gone, and the politics of a large company are gone. Remember that grief I talked about in earlier chapters? It's been replaced with joy, authenticity, and freedom.

Dreams for the Future

Do you want to know what really excites me? The dreams and possibilities I'm building for the future. Sometimes, I catch myself grinning at my computer screen as I plan what's next, and honestly? That never happened in my corporate days.

Next year, I'm aiming to triple both my hotel sourcing and coaching businesses. Not because I need to prove anything but because I genuinely love what I do. I'm planning retreats where women can come together to discover their values, embrace authentic living, and work through growth and grief together. Picture it: A beautiful hotel (that I sourced, of course!), comfy clothes encouraged, Diet Cokes on demand, and real conversations about choosing yourself.

But here's the best part: my dreams aren't just about business growth. I want to travel with my husband just because we can. I'm planning to take my nieces and nephews on more adventures. I'm dreaming up ways to bring more joy to my clients' lives through both my coaching and my event planning. And you know what? None of these dreams feel heavy or anxiety-inducing like my corporate goals used to. They feel light, exciting, and possible.

The Ripple Effect

Perhaps the most beautiful discovery has been watching how choosing joy creates ripples far beyond my own life. Last month, my 10-year-old niece Ellis came home from school bursting with excitement. Her teacher had asked if anyone knew a business owner, and she had proudly raised her hand.

"That's right, isn't it?" she asked me. "You have a business?"

When I confirmed, she asked something no one else had dared: "Do you regret that you quit your job?"

Without hesitation, I replied, "No. I love what I'm doing. I'm learning something new every day. I spend time talking to people who are kind and supportive. *And* I can take time off like this to hang out with you."

A few weeks later, she and her brother, Boston, approached me about starting their own business making bracelets and necklaces. When they made their first $1000 and created their first paid video about being kid entrepreneurs, their pride was contagious. They're not just making money; they're learning that they can create their own lane, just like their aunt did.

Your Path Home

If you're wondering if choosing authenticity over security is worth it, I want you to know something: The road isn't always smooth, but it leads somewhere beautiful. Your version of success might look different than mine, and it should. The key isn't to copy someone else's journey; it's to have the courage to create your own.

Remember:

- Your values are your best business compass
- Authenticity attracts the right opportunities
- True security comes from being aligned with your truth
- Impact and income can grow together
- Joy is a valid business strategy

Sometimes, the bravest thing you can do is trust that being completely yourself is exactly what the world needs. And from where I sit now, in my comfy clothes with my Diet Coke, helping others find their way to authenticity, I can tell you—it's worth every uncertain moment.

Aha! Moment

I was sitting in my home office one morning, looking at my packed calendar—back-to-back meetings, client deliverables due, inbox overflowing. In my corporate life, this kind of day would have left me exhausted and stressed.

But instead, I felt energized. Excited even. That's when it clicked: The work itself hadn't necessarily gotten easier—I still have deadlines, demands, and full days. But because everything I do now aligns perfectly with my values, it energizes rather than drains me.

The difference isn't in the amount of work—it's in the alignment. When you're living and working in sync with your core values, even the challenging days feel purposeful rather than punishing. That's not just joy—that's freedom.

Looking Ahead

As we close this chapter on finding joy, you might be wondering what happens next. What emerges when you've learned to let go, embraced authentic leadership, and discovered unexpected joy? The answer lies in something even more transformative—becoming fully, completely yourself. Not a new version, but rather the truest version of who you've always been.

The world is waiting for your authentic self. Choose you.

Chapter Twelve

Possibilities Practice

Remember when I realized I'd spent years calculating the cost of leaving but never calculated the cost of staying? Sometimes, our biggest possibilities show up when we finally give ourselves permission to dream differently. So grab your favorite drink, get comfy, and let's explore what becomes possible when you write your own rules.

Your Possibilities Practice

Exercise 1: Permission Slips

Time needed: 45 minutes

Remember those permission slips we needed for school field trips? Well, we're writing new ones—but this time, they're from you to you. Think of it like getting a hall pass for your dreams!

Step 1: Create Your Permission Slip (15 minutes)

On a fresh page in your journal (or hey, make it fancy on nice paper if you want!), write:

Success Permission Slip

I, [Your Name], give myself permission to:

- Define success differently at each stage of my life
- Change my mind when something isn't working
- Celebrate wins others might not understand
- [Add your own permissions...]

Step 2: Name What You're Up Against (15 minutes)

Just like I had to face those voices telling me I was crazy to leave before my pension kicked in, let's identify yours:

External Voices to Quiet:

- What do others say about your choices?
- What "shoulds" are you hearing?
- What judgments do you face?

Internal Doubts to Address:

- What fears keep you up at night?
- What old stories are you telling yourself?
- What's holding you back?

Step 3: Write Your Truth (15 minutes)

Complete these statements:

- Success for me means...
- I know I'm successful when...
- My version of success includes...
- I refuse to measure my success by...

End with: "This permission slip is valid starting today and never expires." Sign and date it.

Here is an example of my Success Permission Slip:

I, Kristen, give myself permission to:

- Define success completely differently than my 30-year corporate definition
- Be an incredible aunt and stepmom instead of forcing myself into traditional motherhood

- Accept that my relationship with my stepkids may never look like a Hallmark movie

- Walk away from my pension early and executive title to protect my peace

- Change direction when something isn't working, even if others don't understand

- Combine seemingly unrelated passions (like coaching and event planning) into my own unique path

- Take a Diet Coke run every morning just because it brings me joy

- Measure success by the lives I touch rather than the title on my business card

- Trust that financial security can look different than a corporate retirement plan

- Value peace of mind over status and authenticity over approval

- Start over at 53, knowing my decades of experience aren't wasted but are preparation for what's next

- Create a path that doesn't exist yet, even if others think I'm crazy

External Voices I've Had to Quiet:

- "But you've worked so hard to get here!"
- "No one leaves before their pension kicks in"
- "You'd make such an amazing mom"
- "Isn't it too late to start over?"
- "What about your retirement?"

Internal Doubts I've Faced:

- What if I can't make it on my own?
- Am I throwing away everything I've worked for?
- What if I'm too old to start over?
- Will I regret not having my own kids?
- Who am I without my executive title?

My Truth: Success for me means waking up excited about my day, being fully present for the people I love, and using my experiences to help others find the courage to choose themselves. It means creating meaningful moments with my family, celebrating small wins with my stepkids, and building something that aligns with all of who I am—not just the parts that fit in a corporate box.

This permission slip is valid starting today and never expires.

Signed, Kristen

Dated: The day I chose myself

Now that you've given yourself permission to dream differently (feels good, right?), let's get practical about how we'll measure those dreams.

Exercise 2: Success Metrics Makeover

Time needed: 45 minutes

Remember how I had to let go of measuring success by titles and salary? Let's create new ways to measure what actually matters to you.

Step 1: Audit Current Metrics (15 minutes)

List all the ways you currently measure success:

- Financial (salary, savings, etc.)
- Professional (title, status, etc.)
- Personal (relationship status, possessions, etc.)

For each metric, ask:

- Who chose this measure?
- Does it align with my values?
- How does it serve me?

Step 2: Create New Metrics (15 minutes)

Design metrics that actually matter to you. Here are some examples to get you started.

Energy Metrics:

- Times you felt fully alive
- Moments of genuine excitement
- Days you looked forward to work

Authenticity Metrics:

- Times you spoke your truth
- Moments you chose alignment over approval
- Situations where you honored your values

Impact Metrics:

- Lives you touched
- Genuine connections made
- Positive changes influenced

Joy Metrics:

- Belly laughs shared
- Moments of pure presence

- Times you chose peace over pressure

Step 3: Implementation Planning (15 minutes)

Create your weekly success tracker:

- What will you measure?
- How will you track it?
- When will you review it?
- How will you celebrate progress?

Speaking of keeping it real, let's check in on how authenticity shows up in your world.

Exercise 3: Authenticity Audit

Time needed: 60 minutes

Just like I had to get honest about what wasn't working in my corporate life, this exercise helps you see clearly what needs to change.

Part 1: Current Reality Check (20 minutes)

Rate each area 1-5 (1 = Never true, 5 = Almost always true):

Energy & Connection

___ I feel energized rather than drained after interactions

___ I can be my full self in most situations

___ My relationships feel genuine

___ I speak my truth without fear

Values Alignment:

___ My actions match my values

___ I make decisions based on what matters to me

___ I set boundaries that honor my needs

___ I celebrate authentic wins, not just expected ones

Information Flow

___ Truth moves freely up and down the organization

___ Help is offered without political calculations

___ Resources and information are shared openly

___ Problems are addressed directly, not through back channels

Safety to be Real

___ People readily admit when they don't know something

___ Mistakes are treated as learning opportunities

___ Different perspectives are genuinely welcomed

___ Vulnerability is seen as strength, not weakness

Leadership Behavior

___ Leaders consistently do what they say they'll do

___ Tough messages are delivered directly and compassionately

___ Credit is given accurately and generously

___ Values guide decisions, not just presentations

Team Dynamics

___ Collaboration happens naturally, not by force

___ Conflicts are addressed openly and respectfully

___ People bring their whole selves to work

___ Small wins are celebrated alongside big victories

Part 2: Pattern Recognition (20 minutes)

Look at your three lowest scores and ask:

- What's getting in the way of being real?
- What small step could create more authenticity?
- Who could support this change?
- What permission do you need?

Part 3: Action Planning (20 minutes)

Choose ONE area to focus on this week:

- What will you do?
- When will you do it?

- How will you know it's working?

Remember: Just like my journey from participating in politics to creating authentic spaces, change happens one choice at a time. Start small, be consistent, and celebrate progress. The path to authentic leadership isn't about becoming someone new; it's about having the courage to be who you really are, even when it would be easier not to.

Now that we've got authenticity covered, let's talk about what brings you joy.

Exercise 4: Joy Discovery

Time needed: 45 minutes

Remember how I found joy in those simple Diet Coke runs? Let's map out what brings you that kind of authentic happiness.

Part 1: Joy Signals (15 minutes)

Take a moment to notice:

- What brings unexpected lightness to your day?
- When do you feel most like yourself?
- What makes you smile without trying?
- Where do you feel energy rather than drain?

Part 2: Joy Space (15 minutes)

Look at your calendar for the past week:

- Circle activities that energized you
- Put an X through activities that drained you
- Draw a heart next to moments of pure presence

Ask yourself:

- What patterns do you notice?
- What "shoulds" could you release?
- What boundaries would create more joy?

Part 3: Joy Practice (15 minutes)

Design your daily joy injections:

- What morning practice would feed your soul?
- Who could be part of your joy community?
- How will you celebrate small wins?
- What space needs protecting?

Alright, now that we've covered success, authenticity, and joy, let's dream even bigger.

Exercise 5: Possibility Mapping

Time needed: 60 minutes

This is where we bring it all together and dream up what's next!

Step 1: Dream Zones (20 minutes)

Map out possibilities in four areas:

Work & Impact:

- What work lights you up?
- How do you want to contribute?
- What problems call to you?
- What legacy speaks to your heart?

Relationships & Community:

- Who energizes you?
- What connections feel real?
- How do you want to show up?
- What communities call to you?

Learning & Growth:

- What fascinates you?

- What skills attract you?
- What experiences beckon?
- Where do you want to grow?

Joy & Wellbeing:

- What brings you alive?
- How do you want to feel?
- What adventures appeal?
- What would delight you?

Step 2: Reality Bridges (20 minutes)

For each zone:

- Where are you now?
- Where do you want to be?
- What's one small step forward?
- What support do you need?

Step 3: Action Path (20 minutes)

Create your possibility timeline:

- One tiny step for this week

- One bigger move for this month

- One bold action for this quarter

- One dream for this year

Next Steps

- Post your favorite permission slip somewhere you'll see it daily (mine's on my office wall!)

- Start tracking one new success metric this week

- Practice one authentic choice each day

- Create one small joy ritual

- Plan your first possibility step

- Schedule your first celebration

The world is waiting for your authentic self. Take that first step. Choose you.

Visit www.kristenchimack.com for digital resources and to subscribe to the Kickin' it with Kristen newsletter

Part 4

Integration

"What if every choice to choose yourself, every hard goodbye, every brave new beginning was actually leading you home? This isn't about becoming someone new—it's about remembering who you've been all along."

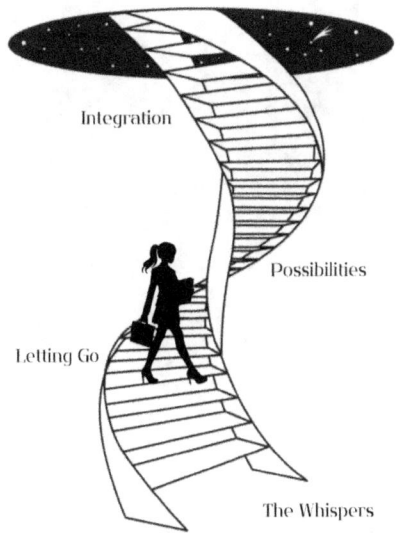

Growth Through Grief Spiral

Chapter Thirteen

Embracing Authenticity

From my earliest memories, authenticity had a face—my grandma Gail. While other grandmas were baking cookies (though she did that too), mine was attending same-sex weddings before they were widely accepted, dreaming about tattoos in her senior years, and teaching us that boredom was impossible because "after all, you have a mind!" Through hours of coloring, creating paper villages, and playing games, she showed me that being yourself wasn't just acceptable—it was essential.

Growing up far from our extended family taught me early lessons about growth and grief. Despite the distance from grandparents, aunts, uncles, and cousins spread across different states, we maintained close connections. Each goodbye brought tears, but also strengthened our bonds. These early experiences shaped how I understood both loss and growth throughout my life.

Authenticity had a different meaning in my family. With them, I always felt being me was perfect. My grandma Gail's influence went far beyond those hours of coloring and creating paper villages. She showed me what it looked like to live without apology, to embrace your true self even when it didn't match others' expectations. Her acceptance of all people, her adventurous spirit, and her way of making everyone feel seen and valued—these weren't just personality traits; they were lessons in authentic living.

When I think back now, the signs of who I really am were always there, woven through every stage of my life. At five years old, I was the kid who loved to play house, explore the neighborhood, and make mud pies—always creating little adventures and experiences for others to join. By thirteen, I was the one organizing everything—from backyard performances to neighborhood games. If something needed planning, somehow, I ended up in charge (though nobody seemed to mind!).

By eighteen, I had become the go-to person for creating experiences for my siblings and friends. Whether it was planning road trips, organizing study groups, or putting together celebrations, I loved bringing people together and making moments matter. I was constantly focused on building memories and, looking back now, already showing signs of that teaching and coaching spirit that would emerge later.

The thread was there all along—this natural pull toward creating experiences, organizing meaningful moments, and helping others navigate their paths. But somewhere along the way, corporate

America had different ideas about who I needed to be and had different lessons to teach.

In my first professional role as a young supervisor, I discovered the complexity of bringing your authentic self to work. Leading a team of twelve people, most at least double my age, I faced a crucial question: What could I possibly offer them? All I knew was how to be me—yet being me seemed to make my boss uncomfortable. That's when the feedback started, and with it, my journey of trying to fit the culture began.

The contrast between these worlds—family and corporate—created an internal tension that would take years to resolve. At home, authenticity was celebrated. At work, it needed to be managed, modified, and molded to fit organizational expectations.

The Corporate Mold

It's sad, really. We talk so much about embracing our authentic selves, yet from a very young age, we're bombarded with messages to be anything but our true selves.

Be more polite. Smile more. Don't be too loud. Speak up. Fit in. Dress like everyone else. Hide your quirks. Follow the trends, not your interests.

And all of that happens before you even make it out of middle school. Then, you enter the professional world, and it only gets worse. You're told to network a certain way, act more corporate, and never let your personal life bleed into your professional one. With all that noise, how can you possibly embrace your authentic self?

The corporate world has a special way of reshaping you. First came the personality tests—Myers-Briggs, DiSC, and Strengths Finder. Each one trying to put me in a box, label my tendencies, and prescribe how I should interact with others. Then came the leadership assessments, 360-degree feedback, and development plans. Every piece of feedback seemed to carry the same message: change who you are to fit what we need.

For most of my career, I thought I was embracing authenticity. But in reality, I was just fitting into the version of authenticity that aligned with the culture of the organization I was in. It was a traditional "good old boy" culture where you had to be tough, distant, and always on. Work was your life. You said "yes" to everything, even when you didn't want to. You worked harder and harder, hoping someone someday might decide you were ready for a promotion.

The Breaking Point

After that pivotal executive meeting, something inside me shattered. The mask I'd carefully constructed over thirty years began to crack. Here I was, being told to prop up an unhealthy situation, to "coach" a struggling leader while hiding the dysfunction. The message was clear: conform or leave.

But conforming wasn't an option anymore. I felt physically ill walking into the office. My anxiety skyrocketed. Sleep became elusive. The disconnect between who I was and who I was expected to be had become too great. I knew I needed to leave, but the question that kept me up at night was: "Now what?"

It's a strange feeling when you've outgrown something but don't know what's next. I had spent decades building this career, this identity. Who was I without it? The thought of leaving terrified me, but staying felt impossible. I was stuck in this uncomfortable in-between, feeling out of alignment with everything I valued.

The contrast between my work life and personal life became painfully clear during family gatherings. One weekend, I was at my niece's cheer competition, fully present, laughing, cheering, and being completely myself. The next day, I was back in the office, carefully measuring every word, managing every reaction, and trying to be what everyone needed me to be. The disparity was exhausting.

My nieces and nephews, in their innocence, would ask questions that cut straight to the heart: "Aunt Kristen, why do you look so tired?" "Why don't you smile as much anymore?" Children have this incredible ability to see through pretense, and their observations were like mirrors reflecting back how far I'd strayed from myself.

Getting Help

It took me months to admit I couldn't figure this out alone. I was too close to it, too wrapped up in the organization's messaging, too isolated in that dysfunctional environment. The voice that had once whispered "choose you" was now screaming, but I needed help hearing what came after that.

That's when I made a decision that would change everything: I hired a coach. Not one the company provided—I needed someone completely outside the system. It might sound like a small step, but for me, it was monumental. It meant admitting I didn't have all the answers. It meant investing in myself instead of just working harder. Most importantly, it meant creating space to explore possibilities beyond the walls of this organization that had defined me for so long.

My coach asked questions that made me squirm, in the best possible way:

- Who are you when you're not being an executive?

- What would you do if you weren't afraid?

- What values are non-negotiable for you?

- When do you feel most alive?

These questions led me back to memories of sitting with Grandma Gail, creating those paper villages. She never asked what practical purpose they served or how they would advance my career. She simply delighted in watching me create, in seeing me fully expressed. When was the last time I had felt that free?

I also joined organizations that could expose me to other industries and help me build a network beyond my corporate bubble. Each of these investments in myself felt both terrifying and liberating. I was spending money to potentially make less money—try explaining that one to your financial planner!

The Journey Back to Me

The work with my coach led me to a deep dive into my core values. This wasn't the corporate version of values—the kind you frame and hang on office walls. This was about discovering what truly mattered to me, what I couldn't live without.

Through readings, exercises, and honest conversations, I began to identify and define my non-negotiables or core values. But these weren't just corporate buzzwords on a wall; they were deeply personal truths that reflected who I am at my core:

Family meant something specific to me: my husband, his kids (who became my bonus kids), our parents (his and mine), our siblings and all their children, plus the extended crew of aunts, uncles, and cousins. It wasn't just about having Sunday dinners or showing up on holidays. It was about being truly present in their lives, being that person they could call at 2 AM just to share exciting news or when life got hard. It meant creating a space where everyone knows they belong, no questions asked.

Courage showed up in unexpected ways in my life. Sure, it was about trying new things, like moving to England for a study abroad program or starting my own business. But it was also about those smaller moments—speaking up in meetings when everyone else was nodding along, sharing unpopular opinions, or simply being comfortable with choices that didn't fit the "normal" path. (Trust me, leaving an executive position to start your own business definitely tests this one!)

Curiosity became my superpower. It meant maintaining that childlike wonder about the world that my Grandma Gail taught me: asking questions without worrying about looking silly, never assuming I knew the whole story, and staying open to learning something new every day. It's what led me to explore new countries, try new experiences, and ultimately, question the status quo in my career.

Transparency became non-negotiable after years of watching office politics and hidden agendas wreak havoc. For me, it meant speaking the truth even when my voice shakes, sharing the hard stuff even when it would be easier to sugar-coat it, and being real about all aspects of my life, the wins and the mess-ups. No more playing the corporate game of saying one thing in meetings and another in private conversations.

Autonomy was my freedom song, the ability to design my life on my own terms. It meant having the flexibility to work when inspiration strikes (hello, 1 a.m. writing sessions!), exploring new ideas without asking permission, and fully being myself without worrying about fitting into someone else's mold.

As these values became clearer, so did the extent of my misalignment. No wonder I felt stuck—I was living in direct opposition to everything I valued most. The organization valued conformity; I valued authenticity. They wanted silence; I valued transparency. They demanded constant availability; I valued family time.

The more I reconnected with my true values, the more my behavior naturally shifted. I started setting boundaries around my time. I spoke up more in meetings, offering honest feedback instead of carefully crafted responses. I shared parts of my personal life—talking about my husband, stepkids, nieces and nephews, the things that made me *me*.

And that's when the feedback started coming:

- "You seem less available lately."

- "You're being too direct."

- "We need you to be more strategic in your communication."

But this time, instead of trying to modify my behavior to fit their expectations, I recognized these comments for what they were—signs that I was finally being authentic. The discomfort others felt wasn't about me being wrong; it was about me no longer playing the role they expected.

Coming Home to Yourself

One Sunday afternoon, I was sitting with my youngest niece, coloring just like I used to do with Grandma Gail. She looked up at me and said, "I like when you're just you, Aunt Kristen." In that moment, I felt the full circle of what authenticity means—from learning it with Grandma Gail to losing it in corporate America to rediscovering it partly through the very next generation.

The path back to authenticity isn't about becoming someone new—it's about remembering who you've always been. It's about peeling back the layers of who you thought you should be to reveal who you are. Sometimes you need help doing that peeling. Sometimes you need permission to be yourself. And sometimes, you need to be reminded of who you were before the world told you to be something else.

For me, embracing authenticity meant reconnecting with that little girl who created paper villages with her grandma. It meant honoring the wife who chooses game nights over fancy parties, who isn't afraid to have hard conversations, and who believes that a strong marriage is built on truth, laughter, and the freedom to be who you are. It meant honoring the aunt who shows up fully present for school events and birthday parties. It meant being the leader who speaks truth, even when it's uncomfortable. Most importantly, it meant choosing myself, over and over again, until being authentic became more natural than being what others expected.

Aha! Moment

A senior leader stopped me in the hallway one morning. "You seem to really like what you're doing. How are things going?" he asked with that familiar corporate smile. I felt that familiar pressure to give the expected response. You know the one: "Everything's great! Love the work, team's fantastic, new boss is bringing such fresh perspective!" Instead, something inside me shifted. Maybe it was the exhaustion of pretending, or maybe it was that recent meeting still fresh in my mind, but I chose truth instead of comfort.

"Actually, I'm having a really hard time," I heard myself say. "I've lost trust in the organization, and honestly, I'm not enjoying the work because of the environment we've created." The shock on his face was immediate. He stammered something about following up, and we scheduled a meeting that would be rescheduled again and again until I resigned nine months later, never having that promised conversation.

That's when it hit me. Authenticity isn't just about speaking your truth; it's about being okay with how others receive it. While that follow-up meeting never happened, something more important did: I had finally chosen being real over being accepted. The cost of that choice was clear: uncomfortable interactions, canceled meetings, and the subtle pulling away of people who preferred the comfortable façade. But the relief of finally being honest? That was priceless. Sometimes, choosing yourself means choosing your truth, even when it makes others uncomfortable enough to avoid you entirely.

Chapter Fourteen

Living Your Truth: The Journey Continues

"Sometimes you have to change everything to find your way back to who you've always been."

I wrote these words in my journal one morning, sitting in my home office wearing yoga pants and a hoodie, hair in a messy ponytail, and no makeup—exactly as I am. The contrast between this moment and my corporate days hit me: no more suits, no more carefully crafted image, no more pretense. Just me, being fully myself, doing work I love. It's like finding a favorite sweater you thought you'd lost, only to discover it fits better than ever.

Remember that Growth Through Grief Spiral we talked about at the beginning of this journey? Well, guess what? It doesn't stop once you make big changes. If anything, it becomes more meaningful as you learn to trust the process.

The Spiral in Action

Let me show you how this works in real life through a recent coaching session. My client—let's call her Ali—was describing a situation that felt eerily familiar. A top performer her entire career, on track for an executive role, suddenly finding herself receiving pointed feedback under new leadership. Her confidence was shaken. The path that had seemed so clear now felt uncertain.

As she spoke, I recognized each phase of the spiral playing out:

The Whisper Phase: Her body was already sending signals—tension headaches, sleepless nights, that familiar Sunday dread.

The Letting Go Phase: She was beginning to question the corporate definition of success she'd always followed.

The Possibility Phase: New options were emerging, even if they felt scary to consider.

The Integration Phase: She was starting to see how this challenge might be leading her toward something more authentic.

Instead of helping her navigate the politics or modify her behavior to meet expectations, I asked her the questions I wish someone had asked me: "What are your values? What does success actually look like to you—not to your leader, not to the organization, but to you?"

Together, we explored two roads: one to improve in her current role authentically and another to explore what else might be possible. Here's what I really want you to know: authentic living isn't just for entrepreneurs or those willing to walk away from corporate life. The road to authentic success has many routes, and I've had the privilege of watching clients find their way on both.

From Politics to Authenticity: A Real-Time Journey

Do you want to know the biggest surprise about building a business based on authenticity? Success comes from genuinely helping others, not from sophisticated marketing strategies or careful image management. This completely flips the traditional corporate mindset on its head.

Let me show you what I mean. Just this morning, I received a message from a hotel partner I've been working with on a complex event: "I love working with you. You're upfront about what the client needs, you understand our needs, and you're down-to-earth, easy to work with...even during tough negotiations. I wish I could work with you on every event."

Reading those words, I felt tears well up. Not because of the compliment itself, but because it confirmed something powerful: when you finally align who you are with what you do, everything changes. The very qualities that had once been labeled as "too direct" or "not political enough" in my corporate life are now my greatest strengths.

What a contrast from my corporate days, where every conversation felt like a strategic move, every relationship a potential political alliance. I'd carefully curate my image, watch my words, and constantly calculate the impact of each interaction. Exhausting doesn't begin to describe it!

Now? My signature networking move is those virtual Diet Coke chats. Yes, that's what they're called on my calendar! I show up as exactly who I am—usually in that comfy hoodie I mentioned—and focus on simple questions, like: "How can I support you?" No hidden agenda, no political maneuvering, just genuine curiosity and a desire to help.

The transformation has been remarkable. Instead of collecting business cards that gather dust, I'm building real connections that create ripple effects of opportunity and impact. Take this story as an example: A potential client reached out about coaching, and after our initial conversation, I realized someone else in my network specialized exactly in what she needed. The old corporate me might have tried to make it work anyway—after all, that would be "good business," right? Instead, I did something that felt both terrifying and absolutely right: I recommended she meet with this other coach first.

Her reaction? Shock, followed by deep appreciation. Not only did she end up working with both of us in different capacities, but she's become one of my biggest referral sources. Why? Because she experienced firsthand what it looks like when someone prioritizes genuine service over personal gain.

Here's how the spiral shows up even in these simple interactions:

- **Whisper:** That intuitive nudge to share freely instead of holding back

- **Letting Go:** Releasing the need to turn every interaction into a sale

- **Possibility:** Opening to unexpected connections and opportunities

- **Integration:** Seeing how authenticity naturally creates success

Finding Peace Through Alignment

Let's talk about what success feels like when you're fully aligned with your values. Yes, my income is less predictable now, but here's what I've gained:

- Sleep that actually restores me

- Mornings without dread

- Energy that lasts all day

- Genuine excitement about my work

- Peace that persists even through challenges

The physical transformation has been remarkable. Remember those tension headaches and constant anxiety from my corporate days? Gone. Even when work is overwhelming (because, yes, that still happens), it's a different kind of stress. It's the productive kind that comes from growth and challenge, not from maintaining a façade or navigating politics.

This peace isn't just for those who leave corporate life. I've worked with many clients who've found similar alignment while staying in their organizations. One client, a senior executive, initially thought she needed to leave her company to find peace. Through our work together, she discovered ways to bring more authenticity to her role. She started leading from her values, having more honest conversations, and creating spaces for her team to be real. Not only did she find the peace she was seeking, but she also became known as the leader everyone wanted to work for.

Aha! Moment

Just last week, I was on a call with a potential client who asked about my biggest failure since leaving corporate life. The old me would have crafted a careful response, turning it into a story of triumph. Instead, I honestly shared about the months of uncertainty, the deals that fell through, and the moments of doubt.

To my surprise, this led to one of the most genuine business conversations I've ever had. We talked about real challenges, shared actual fears, and connected on a human level. By the end of the call, they didn't just become a client—they became part of my authentic community.

That's when it hit me: The Growth Through Grief Spiral isn't just a framework for navigation—it's a pathway back to who we've always been. Each turn brings us closer to our truth, even as it spirals us forward into new possibilities.

Your Journey

As we close this chapter, I want you to know something: Your journey through the spiral will look different than mine, and that's exactly how it should be. Your whispers will be unique to you. Your letting go will follow its own timeline. Your possibilities will emerge in their own way. Your integration will create its own beautiful pattern.

The only constants are:

- Trust the whispers

- Honor the grief

- Welcome the growth

- Keep choosing you

And hey, if you need me, I'll be over here in my comfy clothes, Diet Coke in hand, creating my own kind of success. Maybe our spirals will cross paths someday. Until then, remember:

The world needs your authentic self. Every step toward that truth—no matter how small—is a step worth taking.

Choose you. Again and again.

Chapter Fifteen

The Practice of Integration

Remember how all those seemingly separate choices in my life—from moving to Disney to studying in England to ending that relationship to leaving corporate life—eventually wove together into something that made perfect sense? That's what integration is about. It's not just adding up all the pieces; it's seeing how they create something entirely new.

Integration is a lot like making your favorite recipe. Sure, you could throw everything in at once and hope for the best. But when you take your time, add things in the right order, and really let each ingredient shine—that's when the magic happens. So let's walk through this together, just like I had to figure it out (with maybe a few less mess-ups than I made along the way).

Your Integration Journey

Exercise 1: Values Integration

Time needed: 90 minutes

Remember those core values we discovered earlier—the real ones, not the corporate wall art kind? Let's see how they actually show up in your life.

Step 1: Values in Action Review (30 minutes)

For each of your core values, let's get real about where they're showing up (or hiding):

Current Expression:

- Where does this value naturally shine through?
- Where's it struggling to break free?
- What helps it flourish?
- What's getting in its way?

Future Vision:

- How could this value show up more?
- What needs to shift?
- What becomes possible?
- What support do you need?

Step 2: Integration Planning (30 minutes)

Take each value and break it down like this:

- Today I... (how you're living it now)
- I'm ready to let go of... (what's holding you back)
- Tomorrow I will... (what you want to do differently)
- My next small step is... (one specific action)
- I'll protect this by... (your boundaries)

Here's how I did mine:

Value: Transparency

- **Today I:** Struggle to give straight feedback in meetings
- **I'm ready to let go of:** Making everyone comfortable all the time
- **Tomorrow I will:** Share observations directly but respectfully
- **My next small step is:** Raise one specific concern in tomorrow's meeting
- **I'll protect this by:** Preparing my key points and reminding myself that honest feedback serves everyone

Remember: This isn't about overnight transformation (trust me, I tried that—it doesn't work!). It's about small, consistent choices to be more you. Sometimes, just sharing one honest opinion in a meeting or saying no to something that doesn't align with your values can start a revolution in how you show up.

Exercise 2: Joy Integration

Time needed: 45 minutes

You know what's funny? When I left corporate life, I thought I needed some complicated strategy for success. Turns out that Joy is actually a pretty solid business plan. Let's weave some of that into your daily life.

Step 1: Joy Audit (15 minutes) Let's find your joy sources (no corporate jargon allowed!):

- What makes you lose track of time?
- Who makes you feel energized?
- What work feels like play?
- What simple pleasures make you smile?

Step 2: Joy Integration (15 minutes) Create your joy map:

- Daily joy moments (mine always start with Diet Coke!)
- Weekly joy practices

- Monthly joy adventures

- Quarterly joy celebrations

Step 3: Joy Protection (15 minutes) Because joy needs guardians too:

- What boundaries protect your joy?

- How will you prioritize it?

- What permission do you need?

- How will you defend it?

Exercise 3: Your Integration Action Plan

Time needed: 60 minutes

Remember how I had to figure out how to combine my love for events with my passion for coaching? Let's create your roadmap for bringing everything together.

Step 1: Gather Your Insights (20 minutes) Look back at what we've covered:

- What whispers keep showing up?

- What have you let go of?

- What possibilities light you up?

- What patterns are emerging?

Step 2: Design Your Rhythm (20 minutes)

Create your ideal flow:

Daily Practices:

- Morning rituals
- Energy check-ins
- Boundary maintenance
- Joy moments
- Evening reflection

Weekly Practices:

- Deep work time
- Connection rituals
- Review and adjust
- Celebration habits

Monthly Practices:

- Big picture review
- Course corrections
- Community building

- Growth planning

Step 3: Support System Design (20 minutes)

Build your support crew:

- Who's on your team?

- What resources do you need?

- How will you stay accountable?

- When will you review and adjust?

Exercise 4: Leadership Truth Document

Time needed: 90 minutes

Speaking of bringing it all together, let's capture how you want to show up as a leader. Remember my story about finally getting real with my team? Your turn!

Step 1: Your Leadership Reality (30 minutes)

Get honest about:

Communication Style:

- How do you naturally communicate?

- What can people expect on your good days?

- What about your harder days?

- What promises are you willing to make (and keep)?

Values and Non-Negotiables:

- What values won't you compromise?
- What behaviors won't you tolerate?
- What commitments will you always honor?
- What boundaries need to be clear?

Growth Areas:

- What are you actively working on?
- Where do you need support?
- How should people give you feedback?
- What do you want to learn?

Step 2: Draft Your Document (30 minutes)

Create these sections:

1. "What You Can Count On From Me"
    - Your communication style and promises
    - Your leadership commitments
    - Your growth journey

2. "My Non-Negotiables"

- Clear boundaries
- Absolute expectations
- Core values in action

3. "How to Work With Me"

- Your working style
- Best ways to communicate with you
- Feedback approach

Step 3: Reality Check (30 minutes)

Time to get real:

- What feels scary to share?
- What feels freeing?
- What support will you need?
- How will you share this?

Here's what my Leadership Truth document looked like:

I believe in direct, honest communication—even when it's uncomfortable. You'll never have to guess where you stand with me or decode corporate speak to understand what I'm saying. I've learned through experience that truth-telling, while sometimes challenging, builds the trust we need to do our best work together.

On my best days, you'll find me energetic, creative, and ready to tackle challenges head-on. On my harder days (and yes, I have them), I might be quieter, shorter in my responses or need more processing time. I'll always let share which kind of day it is, and I invite you to do the same.

What you can count on from me:

- I'll speak up for our team, even to senior leadership
- I'll admit when I don't know something
- I'll make space for different perspectives
- I'll address issues directly instead of letting them simmer
- I'll celebrate your wins as enthusiastically as my own

My non-negotiables:

- No throwing team members under the bus
- No politics over performance
- No pretending everything's fine when it isn't
- No sacrificing wellbeing for metrics

Bringing It All Together: Your Integration Blueprint

Time needed: 30 minutes

Now that you've worked through each exercise let's create your personal integration guide that weaves together all the elements we've explored:

Next Steps

1. **Values in Action** (from Exercise 1)

    - Place your Values Integration Plan somewhere visible
    - Schedule your first check-in to review how your values are showing up daily
    - Set calendar reminders for your "next small steps"

2. **Joy Blueprint** (from Exercise 2)

    - Post your joy map where you'll see it daily
    - Block time for your chosen joy practices
    - Set up boundaries to protect your identified joy sources

3. **Integration Rhythms** (from Exercise 3)

- Schedule your daily, weekly, and monthly practices
- Set reminders for regular support system check-ins
- Plan your first celebration milestone

4. **Leadership Integration** (from Exercise 4)

- Share your Leadership Truth Document with key stakeholders
- Schedule regular reviews of your commitments
- Plan how you'll gather feedback on your authentic leadership

Integration is a practice, not a perfection point. Choose ONE thing from each exercise to implement this week:

- **Values:** Pick one value to consciously express tomorrow
- **Joy:** Start your chosen daily joy practice
- **Rhythm:** Implement your morning or evening ritual
- **Leadership:** Share one part of your Truth Document with someone you trust

Just like my journey from corporate executive to entrepreneur, your path to integration will be uniquely yours. Trust the process, celebrate small wins, and keep choosing you.

THE PRACTICE OF INTEGRATION

As you move forward, know that each exercise in this chapter isn't just a one-time task; it's a living practice that grows with you. Let these tools guide you back to who you've always been, one authentic choice at a time.

Visit www.kristenchimack.com for digital resources and to subscribe to the Kickin' it with Kristen newsletter

Conclusion: The Journey Continues

Throughout this book, we've shared those Aha! moments—those sudden flashes of clarity that changed everything. But here's my final Aha! moment to share with you: The biggest revelations often happen in the most ordinary moments. Like that Tuesday morning when I realized I'd been working in my pajamas and favorite hoodie for three hours, feeling more successful than I ever did in my business clothes in my fancy office.

Remember how this started with the executive meeting that changed everything? Well, here I am, on the other side, and let me tell you, the view is pretty amazing. Not because everything's perfect (spoiler alert: entrepreneurship comes with its own brand of chaos), but because for the first time in decades, the person I am on the inside matches the person I show to the world.

Sure, some days, I still miss that steady paycheck. Sometimes, I catch myself missing those office celebrations or team dinners.

But I don't miss the midnight PowerPoint emergencies. The constant political navigation. The negativity. The passive-aggressive behaviors. The Sunday night dread. The feeling that I was always wearing a mask that got heavier by the day.

Throughout this book, we've explored the Growth Through Grief Spiral—sometimes moving through it once, other times cycling back through phases multiple times, each pass bringing new understanding:

The Whispers (even when they make us squirm!)

- Learning to hear that inner voice saying "choose you"

- Recognizing when your body knows before your mind catches up

- Understanding what success really means (spoiler: it's different for everyone)

- Noticing when relationships start shifting (or ghosting—corporate style)

Letting Go (gulp—this is where it gets real)

- Releasing what no longer fits (including that pension—deep breath!)

- Saying goodbye to work "family" (and realizing who sticks around)

- Dropping the corporate mask (messy bun for the win!)

- Making space for what's next (even when "next" is terrifyingly unclear)

Possibilities (where the magic happens)

- Discovering unexpected joy (often in yoga pants)
- Finding authentic leadership (no more midnight PowerPoint emergencies!)
- Building real connections (the kind that celebrate your whole self)
- Creating your own path (corner office optional)

Integration (bringing it all together)

- Coming home to who you've always been
- Living your truth
- Embracing authenticity in all its forms
- Choosing yourself, over and over again

But here's what I really want you to know—what I wish someone had told me while I was stress-eating my way through those final months at work: This growth through grief thing? It's not a one-time deal. It's that spiral staircase where you keep passing the same spots but with a new perspective each time. Each pass brings a new perspective, deeper understanding, and, yes, sometimes more grief. But that's how it should be. Growth isn't linear, and neither is grief. They dance together, leading you home to yourself.

These days, my life looks completely different. I take breaks whenever I want. I work in clothes that actually feel like me. I help others navigate their own transformations and create experiences that matter. The biggest change isn't in what I do; it's in who I allow myself to be.

And those nieces and nephews of mine? They're teaching me as much as I'm teaching them. Watching them run their business with pure authenticity, celebrating their wins (that pellet ice machine purchase was legendary!), they're showing me what's possible when you never learn to doubt yourself in the first place.

So if you're standing at your own crossroads right now, maybe stress-eating your way through a tough decision (been there!), know this:

- Your inner voice knows the way (even if it's whispering under fluorescent lights)

- Grief makes space for growth

- Joy emerges in unexpected places (often in the simplest moments)

- Authenticity attracts authenticity

- Choosing yourself isn't selfish—it's essential (and yes, you can put that on a t-shirt)

Unsent Letters: The Words We Carry

During one of my virtual Diet Coke chats, I met Laura Krauss, author of *The Layoff Cooties: It's Them, Not You: From Rejection to Redirection and Finding Your Ripple Effect Again*. As we talked, we discovered we shared similar experiences with grief during our career transitions.

What really hit home was our conversation about closure—or rather, the lack of it. Laura shared something that would change how I processed my own journey: she had written letters, some never sent, as a way to work through her feelings. Something about that just clicked.

So, inspired by Laura (thank you for sharing this gift with me), here are my unsent letters. They're raw, they're real, and they helped me find my way through the grief to something better.

Dear [Company Name],

Remember me? The executive who always spoke too directly, cared too much, and refused to play the game? I've been thinking about what I'd say to you if we met for a drink.

First, thank you. Yes, really. Thank you for the opportunities, the challenges, the relationships that shaped three decades of my life. Thank you for the lessons—both the ones you meant to teach and the ones you didn't. That toxic environment that finally pushed me to leave? It taught me what I wouldn't tolerate. Those political games? They showed me the value of authenticity.

But here's what I wish you knew: Those values you have painted on your walls? They're not just decorations. "Family," "Integrity," and "Doing the Right Thing"—these aren't just corporate buzzwords. They're promises. And when you break them, you don't just lose good people; you lose pieces of yourself.

Remember how you used to say I was "too much"? Too direct, too passionate, too focused on doing what's right? Turns out, those weren't flaws—they were my superpowers. I just needed to find the right place to use them.

I hope you find your way back to what matters. I hope those values become more than wall art. Until then, I'll be over here, being "too much" and loving every minute of it.

With gratitude for what was and hope for what could be, Kristen

Dear Friends Who Disappeared,

First, let me say—I get it. I really do. When someone leaves the tribe, it gets complicated. Maybe you felt awkward. Maybe you were protecting your own position. Maybe you just didn't know what to say.

Remember all those coffee runs? The late-night text chains? The inside jokes that made tough days bearable? I miss those moments. Not the politics or the pretense, but the real connections we shared beneath all that.

I want you to know something: my door is always open. Not for office gossip or political maneuvering, but for real conversation. The kind we used to have before titles and hierarchy got in the way.

You might be surprised to learn that life on the other side is pretty amazing. Terrifying sometimes, sure, but in the best possible way. There's room over here for authenticity, for being human, for choosing yourself.

And if you ever find yourself hearing that whisper to choose you? Know that you've got a friend who understands the journey. I'll save you a Diet Coke.

With hope and understanding, Kristen

Dear Past Kristen,

Oh girl, I see you there in your work clothes and perfect makeup, trying so hard to be what everyone needs. I see you calculating the cost of leaving, but never calculating the cost of staying. I see you building walls to protect yourself while wondering why you feel so alone.

You're going to be okay. Better than okay, actually. All those things you think are your biggest weaknesses? Your directness, your passion, your refusal to settle for "good enough"? They're actually your greatest strengths. You just need to find the right place to use them.

That whisper you keep hearing? The one saying "Choose you"? Listen to it. It knows the way home.

Yes, leaving will be hard. You'll cry in your car more times than you can count. You'll question everything. You'll have moments of pure panic. But here's what you need to know: on the other side of that fear is freedom. Real, messy, beautiful freedom.

Remember that little girl who loved creating experiences and bringing people together? She's still in there. And she's been waiting for you to find your way back to her.

The path ahead isn't straight. It spirals and curves and sometimes feels like it's leading you in circles. But each turn brings you closer to who you're meant to be.

Trust yourself. Choose you. The rest will fall into place.

With love from the other side of fear, Future Kristen

P.S. Stock up on Diet Coke. Trust me on this one.

A Final Note

The ending looks nothing like I thought it would. I want you to know something: my door is always open. And that's exactly how it should be. Because this isn't really an ending at all; it's a return to the beginning, to who we've always been.

Maybe our paths will cross someday—at a coffee shop, in a virtual meeting, or at one of my retreats. Maybe you'll share your story of choosing yourself, of growing through grief, of finding your way home. I'll be the one with the Diet Coke, ready to listen.

Until then, remember: You don't have to become someone new. You just have to find your way back to who you've always been. The world is waiting for your authentic self.

Choose you.

About the Author

Kristen Chimack, a former Fortune 50 executive, embodies the courage to choose oneself. Over her 30-year career, she rose from payment clerk to executive, navigating diverse roles in finance, HR, sales, and more. Despite her success, Kristen felt the pull for something more authentic, leading her to leave a six-figure role to found Down-to-Earth Insights LLC.

From childhood, Kristen was drawn to creating experiences and organizing meaningful moments. Whether planning neighborhood games or road trips, she naturally brought people together, making lasting memories. This innate ability to connect and inspire others was always there, woven through every stage of her life. However, corporate America had different ideas about who she needed to be, teaching her lessons that ultimately led her back to her true self.

Today, through coaching, creating experiences with retreats, and hotel sourcing, Kristen empowers others to embrace their potential and redefine success on their own terms. She actively shares insights about choosing yourself and authenticity through daily LinkedIn posts while building meaningful connections with her network. Her weekly newsletter, "Kickin' it with Kristen," delivers Aha! Moments and mid-week motivation to her growing community.

Kristen lives in Illinois with her husband, Mike, where they cheer on Chicago sports teams and treasure afternoons at Wrigley Field. A self-proclaimed Super Aunt, she creates unforgettable experiences with her nieces and nephews. When not transforming lives through her work, you might find her enjoying a Law and Order: SVU marathon.

Connect with Kristen to start your journey: **visit:** www.kristenchimack.com, email **kristen@kristenchimack.com**, or find her on LinkedIn for daily insights and her weekly "Kickin' it with Kristen" newsletter.

Visit www.kristenchimack.com for digital resources and to subscribe to the Kickin' it with Kristen newsletter